STUDENT EDITION

JOHNNY DEROUEN

Published by Life Bible Study

Life Bible Study LLC is a Christian publisher serving churches and Christian
communities in order to advance the Gospel of Jesus Christ, making disciples as we
go.

© 2017 Life Bible Study
Christ by Johnny Derouen
Reprinted from the first edition text, *Christ: The Life of Christ—The Basis of Faith*
(2008), by Clarity Publishers.

All rights reserved. No part of this publication may be reproduced, stored in a
retrieval system, or transmitted in any form or by any means, electronic, mechanical,
photocopying, recording, or otherwise, without the prior permission of Life Bible
Study. Address all correspondence to
Life Bible Study LLC, 5184 Caldwell Mill Road, Suite 204-221, Hoover, AL
35244.

ISBN-13: 978-1-63204-068-8
ISBN-10: 1-63204-068-9
LifeBibleStudy.com

All Scripture quotations, unless otherwise indicated, are taken from the *Holy
Bible: New International Version®*. NIV®. Copyright ©1973,1978, 1984 by the
International Bible Society. Used by permission of Zondervan. All rights reserved.

Printed in the United States of America
1 2 3 4 5 6 / 22 21 20 19 18 17

CHRIST

STUDENT EDITION

TABLE OF CO

ITENTS

HIS IDENTITY IN SCRIPTURE

MEMORY VERSE:

"The Word became flesh and made his dwelling among us. We have seen his glory, the glory of the one and only Son, who came from the Father, full of grace and truth." (John 1:14)

INTRODUCTION

Get ready! You're about to embark on the greatest adventure of your life. For the next year, you'll get to know—in a very personal way—the most amazing man who ever walked the face of the earth: Jesus Christ. He's amazing because of who He actually is—the God of the universe who created all things with just a spoken word. He became man so humankind could know Him. He designed you specifically for an exciting purpose. He wired you with a deep craving to know Him.

Why is it so vital that you take time to look at Jesus Christ? That's easy. The more you know Him, what He's like, and why He does and says what He does and says, the more you'll fall in love with Him and trust Him. You'll be ready to do what He calls you to do. You'll be able to live the adventures for which He created you.

The adventure begins in the following pages. Once you take an in-depth look at this amazing God, you'll never be the same.

Over the next year, you'll have the opportunity to spend time with the God of the universe—just you and Him—as He speaks to you personally through His Word and His Spirit. I encourage you to write down your thoughts in the Journal Space to help you remember everything God reveals to you. Now grab your Bible and get ready to take an up-close and personal look at the God who created you, designed you, loves you, and gave His all for you as we get intimate with Jesus Christ.

DAY 1

Scripture testifies about Jesus. The word testify means to "make a statement based on evidence or proof" or "to give evidence." Jesus said that as you read Scripture, it will show evidence or proof of who He is. Why? So you'll come to know Him and to experience life the way you were designed to live it—to the fullest!

Our main purpose in reading the Bible is to see the evidence of who Jesus is, to know Him, and to experience real life by coming to Him. As you get to know Jesus better by reading God's Word, you'll trust Him more with your life and learn to obey Him. Then real life begins. The challenge is whether or not you believe Jesus is who He says He is. If you do, then what will you do with this knowledge?

As you begin this very personal journey to "diligently study the Scriptures" in order to know Jesus better, what's one question you'd like answered about Jesus or one thing you'd like to discover?

Why doesn't everybody turn to Jesus?

DAY 2

John 1:1-5, 14

This is some pretty heavy stuff. John told us that Jesus is "the Word." He rules all things. He made all things. He is life itself. In fact, life doesn't exist without Him.

Jesus is light to all people. He is God. He actually became flesh so we could know what God is like. This is the One you're choosing to spend a few minutes with each day. Is it worth the sacrifice? Take a moment and ask Jesus to help you know Him deeper as you study His life.

Read John 1:1-5, 14 again. What one aspect of who Jesus is speaks to you the most now? Why?

Would anything in your life cause you to choose to stay in darkness, as described in verse 5? How would you explain that excuse?

Write down the name of one person with whom you'd like to share Jesus. Pray for an opportunity to show Jesus to that person.

DAY 3

Colossians 1:15-18

Write what Colossians 1:15-18 says Jesus has done.

Now you're beginning to understand who this Jesus really is. Read the verses again. Be silent and let the truth of those verses sink into your mind.

Jesus leaves no other option as to who He says He is. He doesn't claim to be a great teacher or a great man. He claims to be God, the Maker and Sustainer of all things—including you. Think about what this means. This truly magnificent God loves you. You're important to Him. As verse 18 clearly states, He wants supremacy in your life so He can guide you to become what He created you to be.

Take a moment and praise (give value to) God.

Write down one thought based on what you just read.

DAY 4

Isn't it amazing to realize that our awesome God reconciled with us through Jesus? This means God restored our friendship with Him. In spite of whatever you've done wrong, Jesus has paid the price to rescue you. You cannot do one bad thing that He hasn't already paid for with His death and resurrection. And He did this so you can come to really know Him. Thus, your challenge is to accept the adventure of spending a few moments each day getting to know Jesus better.

How does it make you feel to know what Jesus did for you?

Take a few moments and thank God for what He's done for you in spite of the circumstances that may be occurring in your life.

DAY 5

Philippians 2:5-11

Talk about a challenge. This Scripture passage encourages every person to develop the same attitude that Jesus possessed. Now how do you do that? Obviously, by your choices and through the power of God in your life (assuming you've made the choice to become a Christian).

Servanthood and humility are two words that come to mind as we read about Jesus' attitude. Since He's all-powerful (as we've already read in Scripture these last four days), He chose to set aside His nature as God to be obedient and die for our sins. Why? So God's name would be honored as people like you and me yield our lives to Him and allow Him to live through us.

Write down at least five different aspects of Jesus' character or five of His actions that show us His humility and obedience to God the Father.

What part of your attitude is the most difficult to yield to God, yet the most necessary if you're to begin developing Jesus' attitude in your life?

HIS ARRIVAL FORETOLD

MEMORY VERSE:

"For to us a child is born, to us a son is given, and the government will be on his shoulders. And he will be called Wonderful Counselor, Mighty God, Everlasting Father, Prince of Peace." (Isaiah 9:6)

INTRODUCTION

As you seek to know Jesus better, you'll discover God has a plan to deliver from a life of sin all who place their faith in his Son. In fact, the word Messiah means "expected deliverer"—Jesus Christ.

From the beginning of time, God set His plan in motion—a plan to bring people back after they chose to live apart from Him. The cool thing is that God is truly sovereign; this means He's in total control of history. We can have great confidence since He's in control—even when things feel as though they're spinning out of control.

Here are a few tidbits to get you excited about God's awesome sovereignty. The Old Testament contains nearly 300 references, called prophecies, about the coming of Jesus Christ. These prophecies give us nearly 300 facts that had to be fulfilled in one person to confirm that He was truly the Messiah. Guess what? All of these were fulfilled in Jesus Christ. (For a detailed list of these prophecies, check out Josh McDowell's book, *The New Evidence That Demands a Verdict*.) The chance for anyone to fulfill just eight of these nearly 300 prophecies is 1 in 100,000,000,000,000,000 (that's one in a quadrillion).

Let's illustrate this. Cover the entire state of Texas with silver dollars piled two feet deep. Mark just one of these silver dollars and drop it anywhere. Now blindfold one man and ask him to choose the marked silver dollar— in one try. This is equivalent to the chance of one man fulfilling only eight of the prophecies. Jesus fulfilled almost 300. God wanted us to know that Jesus is the Messiah. Now let's continue our adventure.

DAY 1

Isaiah 9:2, 6–7

You just read one of the many prophecies God gave His people through the prophets. They promised the Messiah would come and be a "light" to those who walk in darkness. He'd be the final sacrifice for the sins of humankind. Talk about faith! During the Old Testament times, people gained salvation by putting their faith in the Messiah (Jesus Christ) who hadn't come to earth yet. But we can build our faith on an act of God that took place in the past—the death and resurrection of the Christ. All 300 of the Old Testament prophecies were given to assure the Israelites they'd know when the real Messiah came. Since we already know the prophecies came true, we can trust all that God promises us in His Word. What a relief!

How does Isaiah 9:6–7 describe the Messiah? Write down some of the words.

Isaiah 7:14 calls the Messiah "Immanuel," which means "God with us." In other words, Jesus, the Messiah, is literally God with us— God chose to come live in and through us.

What does it mean to know that when you asked Jesus to come into your life, God put His Spirit in you and will be with you wherever you go?

HIS IDENTITY IN SCRIPTURE

DAY 2

Genesis 3:15; Malachi 3:16; Ephesians 6:12-13

You just read some pretty tough verses. God wants you to know that not only does He have an eternal plan for you, but there's also a spiritual battle going on between God's people and Satan's legion of rebellious angels. This is a real battle.

Those who aren't Christians, and even Christians who've turned away from following Jesus, can prevent you from becoming who God made you to be. Your decision to rely upon God and His Word is critical. Malachi 3:16 reveals that people who had a tremendous desire to serve God spent time together for encouragement and to honor God.

One of the greatest challenges for students involves their friendships. Satan often uses our friends to drag us down. He convinces us that since everyone else is doing something, then it must be all right. This is his way of trying to stop us from serving Christ fully.

What kinds of friends do you spend most of your time with? Are they a positive influence on your walk with Jesus?

Are your closest friends growing in their faith in Christ? Pray that God will help you become more sensitive to the types of friendships you choose.

What relationships do you need to pray about?

DAY 3
Micah 5:2

God prophesied through Micah that the Messiah would come from a small clan of Judah and be born in the small, unimportant town of Bethlehem. God's plans are precise. God uses all kinds of people, but He seems to have a specific use for what appears to be unimportant. In the same way, God's eternal plan involves you—no matter how unimportant you may believe you are. God wants you to yield all of your life to Him each day.

How serious are you about knowing Jesus?

Are you willing to continue spending time with Him and His Word each day?

Write about a few areas of your life in which you know God has control and a few areas that you tend to hold back from God. If you're willing, then spend a few minutes with God and yield those areas to God—or explain why you won't. Remember, God knows your heart.

DAY 4
Isaiah 49:14-16

You're an important part of God's eternal plan. Even when you feel forgotten, He remembers you. Isaiah 49:15 reminds us that a mother can forget her child—it happens occasionally—but God will never forget you. Many people write things on their palms, but the ink will eventually rub off. God didn't just write your name on the palm of His hand—He engraved it. You're always on His mind.

Thank God that He never forgets you. Write about a time when you felt God wasn't near.

No matter how you feel, what does God's Word say in Isaiah 49:14-16? Feelings cannot be trusted. Living by faith means learning to trust God's Word.

DAY 5
Isaiah 53:1-7

Ouch! The first seven verses of Isaiah 53 described in clear detail the pain Jesus endured for us. Read verses 5-7 again. In spite of being crushed for our sakes, bearing our sins, and never opening His mouth to complain, people (that's us) still turned away from Him.

Write your thoughts about this.

Part of God's eternal plan was for the Messiah (Jesus) to be crushed for our sins. What love and justice! Without paying the cost ourselves, we can go directly to God because of Jesus. As you pray, thank God for His pursuit of you and for Jesus' great sacrifice.

What response will you make today to Jesus?

MARY'S REACTION OF PRAISE

MEMORY VERSE:

"For the Mighty One has done great things for me—holy is his name." (Luke 1:49)

INTRODUCTION

We do love Christmas! For the next two weeks, our adventure will take us back to that first Christmas—before lighted trees, presents, eggnog, and football bowl games. No matter what time of year it is, that first Christmas will point us to Jesus and His plan for our lives.

How much do you know about Christmas? See if you can answer the following questions: (The correct answers are at the bottom of the page—but don't peek!)

1. In the song "White Christmas," what do the children listen for?
2. What does the word "noel" mean?
3. According to the Bible, how many wise men came to see Jesus?
4. Where did the wise men find Jesus?
5. Which of the four Gospels—Mathew, Mark, Luke, and John— record the birth of Jesus?

To grow in our understanding of Jesus, we must go back to that first Christmas where God literally stepped into human history.

(5) Matthew and Luke.
(1) Sleigh bells in the snow; (2) Christmas; (3) It doesn't give a number; (4) In a house;

DAY 1

Luke 1:26-38

This could be one of the most awesome sections in the entire Bible. Read it again and write down anything that amazes you.

How about these?

> *An angel came down to Mary and said something like, "Hey, you are highly favored, and God is with you!" (v. 28)*

> *Since God favored Mary, He chose her to give birth to the Messiah—as a virgin. She obviously had some questions about exactly how this would happen! (vv. 30-34)*

> *The angel told her not to be afraid—the Holy Spirit would conceive a child inside of her. He also reminded her that nothing is impossible with God (vv. 35-37). That statement alone is worth remembering and repeating.*

Mary, who probably was a teenager, knew the heartache she'd face one day, and she responded with trust. She said she was the Lord's servant and He was free to do with her life whatever He desired.

Learning from a fellow teenager, what's your response as God calls you to trust and obey Him in all areas of your life? Ask God to do whatever He needs to do to build your faith.

DAY 2

Luke 1:39-45

What goes through your mind when you think about Christmas? Luke 1:39-45 records the very first response (other than Mary's) to Christmas. A baby who was still inside his mother's womb leaped for joy. Then his mother, Elizabeth, encouraged Mary that she was indeed carrying the Messiah. Shouldn't we all respond this way— leaping for joy at the birth of Jesus, the Savior, who allows us to have a personal relationship with God?

So far in your life, what's been the hardest thing that God has asked you to do?

Or what's the hardest truth in the Bible for you to obey? What did you learn from that experience?

What would help you trust God more in the tough areas of life?

Spend a few moments with God and tell Him how you feel about your relationship with Him. Then ask God to develop in you a joy about who He is that will last even when tough times come. (And they will come; that's how we grow.)

DAY 3
Luke 1:46-55

You've just read the first Christmas carol ever written. Mary—the teenager chosen by God to be the mother of Jesus—first responded to her responsibility with obedience. Her second response was to tell others (Elizabeth). And her third response was to write a song of thanks and praise to God.

Write down a few of the things for which she praised God.

So what do Mary's responses mean for you and me? Actually, her calling from God is similar to ours. As Jesus' earthly mother, she was chosen by God to physically bring Him into the world. After we become Christians, God gives us the responsibility—and the honor—of spiritually bringing Jesus to those with whom we come in contact. As Jesus is birthed in us, we bring Him into the world around us.

Have you privately responded to God with your willingness to obey? How?

Who do you want to tell about what Jesus has done in your life? When?

MARY'S REACTION OF PRAISE

DAY 4

Matthew 1:18-25

The initial response of Joseph, Mary's fiancé, was quite different than Mary's response. Read verses 18-19 again. Joseph didn't believe Mary initially. Jewish law stated that if a woman who was engaged to be married committed adultery, then the man could publicly disgrace her and have her stoned to death. This was a serious situation. But God revealed to Joseph that what Mary told him was true. Joseph responded with trust and obedience to the Lord.

Many times words alone don't convince others that salvation and life are found only in Jesus. However, God's Spirit can use our words to open someone's heart and mind to who He really is. Our job is to draw people to Him by our lives and words.

If you're struggling with doubts about Jesus, ask God to open your heart and mind to the truth of who He is.

DAY 5

Psalm 139:13–16

Mary was an ordinary teenager, yet God chose her to accomplish great things. Today, God still looks for ordinary people who are willing to trust Him with their lives to accomplish great things. Psalm 139:13-16 reminds us that God created, designed, and crafted each of us especially for what He wants us to do. In fact, you were wired to know God and make Him known. Nothing else will really satisfy you.

Read today's passage again and meditate on what it says to you. The real Christmas question is, "What will you do with this Jesus?"

How does it make you feel to know that God created you to know Him and make Him known?

Choose a personal way to express praise to God. Take some time to praise Him.

HE IS THE GIFT

MEMORY VERSE:

"Today in the town of David a Savior has been born to you; he is the Messiah, the Lord." (Luke 2:11)

INTRODUCTION

Gifts are great! And the best gift-giving time of the year is Christmas. In fact, the greatest gift ever given was God's gift of Jesus. It expressed, once and for all, God's great love for humanity (John 3:16).

As with all gifts, people respond to God's gift in a variety of ways: some with joy, some with disgust, some with apathy ("So what?"), some with fear, some with doubt, and some with rebellion. Our journey this week will examine the circumstances surrounding Jesus' birth and people's responses to it.

Saint Nicholas was an actual person who was so inspired by the birth of Jesus that he spent his life serving others. His reputation for generosity spread throughout the region (now known as Turkey) where he lived during the third and fourth centuries. The story of how he disguised himself and offered presents to needy children spread among the people of Nicholas' day. According to legend, Nicholas gave all that he had while living a life of poverty.

Over the years, people have embellished the story of St. Nicholas, giving him a red suit, nine reindeer, a sleigh, and a North Pole address. The real history of the man has been obscured, but what matters is that the story of St. Nicholas offers us an example of a heartfelt response to Christ's birth. Because he lived a Christ-like life, Nicholas touched the whole world. That same Christ-like mindset and servant-oriented lifestyle are how we're supposed to respond to the birth of Jesus.

This week, we'll look at some different responses to the world-changing event of Christ's birth.

What is your response?

DAY 1

Luke 2:1-7

Our first stop is at the home of the innkeeper who had no room for Mary and Joseph. Imagine God—the Savior of the world—being born right under the nose of the innkeeper. His response?

"Sorry, but I don't have any more rooms. The inn is full."

Yes, I know the words of the innkeeper were never officially recorded. But we can make an educated guess about what he said. He probably wasn't mean. He may have been very polite even. Isn't that a lot like us?

"Jesus, You're great and all, and I'm really glad You're here. But right now my life is just too full of other activities and relationships to make room for You. I'll come see You on Sundays, though—and maybe Wednesdays."

Does that sound like you?

Jesus wants to be Lord of all of you. What should you do to make room for Jesus?

What is God saying to you today?

HE IS THE GIFT

DAY 2

Luke 2:8-20

The shepherds! What a great bunch of guys...just hanging around with sheep, singing, and waiting in a field for the angels to appear. Not true! They were actually the bottom of the food chain in Jewish life. It was a dirty, lonely, low-paying, and disrespected job. But they were the first ones (in fact, the only ones) to whom the angel of the Lord appeared with the good news of the birth of Jesus, the Messiah. They even received a full-fledged concert given by the entire praise band of heaven.

Those shepherds were probably both scared half to death and pumped with joy. Their first response was, "Let's go to Bethlehem and see what this is all about!" Then after they met Jesus, they did two awesome things. First, they told others what they'd seen and heard about Jesus (v. 17). Second, they glorified and praised God (v. 20). Shouldn't this be our response as well?

If you're a Christian, how did you respond in the first few weeks after you became a Christian?

What is God telling you to do today in response to your time with Him?

DAY 3

Luke 2:19, 21-24, 33, 39-40

This is an exciting part of Scripture—how Mary and Joseph responded to Jesus' birth. It's a perfect example of how we should respond to Christ being born in us when we become Christians: (1) Verse 19—Mary treasured and pondered these things. That means she valued her relationship with Jesus as a treasure, and she pondered or thought deeply about it; (2) Verses 21-24—Mary and Joseph obeyed the Law of the Lord and had Jesus consecrated; (3) Verse 33—Mary and Joseph marveled at what was said about Jesus; (4) Verses 39-40—Mary and Joseph returned home and helped Jesus to grow in wisdom and strength.

Shouldn't those be our responses as well?

1. *Make Him the treasure of our lives and think about what that means.*
2. *Obey the Law of the Lord, make public our decision to become a Christian, and be baptized.*
3. *Learn who Jesus is and how to know Him better.*
4. *Develop a daily lifestyle to walk with Jesus.*

What are you committed to doing on a daily basis that will help you achieve God's purpose for your life?

What is God saying to you based on today's passage?

DAY 4

Matthew 2:3-5, 16

Many people respond to the good news of Jesus as King Herod did (and all of Jerusalem with him): It disturbs and angers them.

"How can Jesus be the only way? How intolerant! I refuse to give control of my life over to Jesus—or to anyone else for that matter!"

Others ridicule those who follow Jesus. And still others go even further and physically harm Christians. For more than 2,000 years, people have attempted to stop the spread of the gospel, but it continues to spread. And lives continue to change.

Some people are afraid Jesus will take away their freedom if they trust Him. But once they realize who He really is, they'll say, "Why did I wait so long?"

Ask God to break your heart for the people who are afraid of what Jesus might want from them. Ask Him for a divine appointment to represent Jesus to one fearful person by this time tomorrow.

DAY 5

Matthew 2:1-2, 9-12

The Magi, or wise men, were an interesting bunch of guys. Most theologians believe they were astrologers from Persia or Arabia. They'd heard prophecy of the Messiah, and they'd seen the star in the east. They came to see if it really led to a king. If all they'd heard was true, then they wanted to worship Him.

Many people responded to the birth of Jesus with an honest search to see if Jesus really was who He claimed to be. There's room in the Christian life for honest doubts—doubts that lead to the truth. It's all right to ask questions and seek the truth. Just be sure your search for answers isn't just an excuse to avoid the truth.

What are one or two doubts about the Christian life that you have at this moment?

Who will you go to for help in answering these doubts?

Ask God to teach you about your specific doubts. Be willing to obey God based on what you discover.

HIS ADOLESCENCE

MEMORY VERSE:

"And Jesus grew in wisdom and stature, and in favor with God and man.'"
(Luke 2:52)

INTRODUCTION

Sometimes it's hard for me to imagine that Jesus had parents. How do you parent the Son of God? And how does God in the flesh honor His parents' authority? This week we'll take a look at how Jesus responded to His earthly parents. This will be one of the most important parts of your journey to deepen your relationship with Jesus.

Your parents were put into your life for several reasons:

1. *They see the real you no one else sees. They're the first ones to see if your walk with Jesus is real or if you only put on a front. Whenever you come home, you take off your mask and the real you comes out.*

2. *They're supposed to model godly character for you. Believe it or not, the majority of us will eventually take on most of the characteristics of our parents. That's good news if you have godly parents, and it's something you'll have to resist if your parents haven't been good role models.*

3. *God gives parents a unique ability to discern danger for their children. If you'll learn to listen to them objectively, then God will use them to protect you from destructive relationships and situations.*

4. *Most parents love their children and desire the best for them. All children desire a heart connection with their parents and need that relationship to be healthy.*

If you don't live with your parents or if your parents have failed to fulfill their God-given responsibilities, then God will be your Parent. In fact, many of the Old Testament men and women whom God used were orphans or from one-parent families.

Okay, let's get ready for a week of learning more about Jesus. Remember, He designed you, and He knows how you're wired. Ask God to give you an open heart as He teaches you from His Word this week.

DAY 1
Luke 2:41-50

It's difficult to imagine God having to yield to His earthly parents' authority. In the passage you just read, Jesus didn't stay with His parents. After three days of searching, they finally found Him in the temple. Then Jesus honestly told them He had to do the will of God.

A misunderstanding (common among parents and teenagers) took place, yet Jesus never raised His voice. The important thing is not that misunderstandings happen between you and your parents; the important thing is your response to them. God will use conflicts and trials to help you grow. It's almost like a test. Tests reveal both what you know and what you don't know.

Write down some of the weak areas in your relationship with your mom or dad.

Spend a few moments taking these areas to God and asking Him to improve them. Also, ask God to give you wisdom this week in relating to your parents.

DAY 2

Luke 2:49-52

Yesterday, we learned that Jesus had a misunderstanding with His earthly parents. Parents and teenagers often say really dumb things to each other. But when Jesus' parents corrected Him, He responded in four ways: (1) He listened to what His parents had to say. (2) He didn't raise His voice; He calmly explained His position. (3) Even though they didn't understand Him, He was obedient to them and went home. (4) He desired to learn and grow in wisdom.

Which of these four responses is the most difficult for you to do with your parents? Why?

Ask God to give you opportunities to grow in your relationship with your parents.

DAY 3

Ephesians 6:1-3

Your family relationships are very important to God. In fact, honoring your parents is the first commandment that comes with a promise—that your life will go well and you'll have a successful (long) life.

Pray over these practical ways to contribute to a better relationship with your parents:

- Seek your parents' forgiveness when you're wrong.
- Cooperate with your parents. Ask them what weak areas they see in your life.
- Tell your parents you love them.
- Thank them for all they've done for you.
- Be quick to listen. Try to understand where they're coming from.

Which of these suggestions is the most difficult?

Spend a few moments praying for your parents. Ask God to give them wisdom. Ask God to bring joy in their relationships with you, with each other, and with Him.

DAY 4

Colossians 3:20

Yes, as hard as it seems, God commands you to obey your parents and other authority figures unless the situation leads you to disobey God (Acts 5:27-29). It takes discipline to obey, but discipline (learning to obey God in spite of your feelings) is a strength you'll need throughout your life.

Here are three ways to improve your relationship with your parents. Pray over each one.

Avoid raising your voice with your parents. Proverbs 15:1 teaches that a shouting match will only lead to hurt feelings. Example: "Okay, Mom, I hear what you're saying, but I still don't understand," or "I'm upset right now. Can I calm down first and talk to you about this later?"

Never do anything to betray your parents' trust. Once you do something to make them question your honesty, it's very difficult to regain their confidence.

Take an interest in your parents' lives. It will astound them. Ask them about their jobs, hobbies, or friends. Ask them about their teenage years—dating, school, and the dumb things they did. You might find they're more interesting than you ever imagined.

Spend a few minutes thanking God for your parents.

Write down what God is trying to teach you about your parents.

DAY 5

Proverbs 15:5; Romans 13:1–3

Fool is a terrible name to call someone. Yet this is the word used for a son who spurns his parents' discipline. Even if your parents fail you, God will not. He'll bring other authority figures into your life. My own father was not a believer, and he passed away when I was a young adult. (He received Christ on his deathbed.) God then brought my father-in-law into my life. God has used him in tremendous ways to build me into the person God wants me to be. God will do the same for you if you yield your life to Him.

Parents have a unique ability to see people and circumstances that will do us harm. They've already made mistakes and learned lessons from which we can benefit.

What's one thing you're thankful for about your parents or other authority figures?

What's one lesson God has taught you through your parents or other authority figures?

Spend a few moments thanking God for your parents or other authority figures in your life. Ask Him to continue to bless their lives.

WEEK 6
JOHN THE BAPTIST'S MESSAGE

MEMORY VERSE:

"Truly I tell you, among those born of women there has not risen anyone greater than John the Baptist; yet whoever is least in the kingdom of heaven is greater than he." (Matthew 11:11)

INTRODUCTION

Of all humankind, excluding Jesus, who is the greatest person ever? Jesus said in Matthew 11:11 that no one born of women was greater than John the Baptist. What made John such a special person? What can we learn from John about Jesus' desire for our lives?

This week our journey will take us alongside John the Baptist as we learn from the man who ate locusts and honey and wore clothes made from animal skins. I don't know about you, but camel-hair shirts and underwear don't exactly appeal to me. Even so, Jesus had high regard for John the Baptist, and He considered John a person from whom one could learn a lot.

John wasn't the most popular or gifted person around. In fact, you'll find that God tended to use people we might consider inadequate. God's main stipulations for being used by Him are obedience and willingness.

Take a look at these inadequate people God used in spite of their inadequacies:

- *Moses stuttered.*
- *John Mark was rejected by Paul.*
- *Hosea's wife was a prostitute.*
- *Jacob was a liar.*
- *King David had an affair.*
- *Abraham was too old.*
- *David was too young.*
- *Solomon was too rich.*
- *James and John were self-centered.*
- *Naomi was a widow.*
- *Moses was a murderer.*
- *Jonah ran from God.*
- *Gideon and Thomas doubted.*
- *Jeremiah was depressed and suicidal.*
- *Martha was a worrywart.*
- *Noah got drunk.*
- *Peter had a short temper.*

Well, you get the idea. What's your excuse?

Matthew 3:1-6

Who was John the Baptist? Well, he wasn't the man who founded the Baptist church. He was called "the Baptist" because he preached baptism as a public statement of one's repentance. John was the son of Elizabeth and Zechariah (a Jewish priest). Elizabeth was a relative of Mary, which made Jesus and John the Baptist cousins. (Remember back in Week 3 when we read how a baby leaped in his mother's womb when Mary entered the house? That was John!)

Before John's birth, God chose him to call people to repentance and prepare the way for the Messiah. Even so, John had to choose to obey God's will. His simple lifestyle was a clear sign to the people not to build their lives around what cannot last. The first lesson about Jesus came from John the Baptist: Jesus wants your will.

Write down what God is telling you about your will and His will.

Yielding our will to Jesus is a daily commitment. That means we must choose to give it over to God each day. Start the day by spending some time with God and choosing to trust Him enough to yield your will to Him.

DAY 2

Luke 3:3-8

John the Baptist's mission was to prepare the way of the Lord (Jesus). He preached the coming of the Messiah—great news for Jewish people who were looking forward to His coming. It's also great news for anyone looking for truth and meaning in life today. The same God who called John the Baptist to prepare the way of the Lord is calling us to do the same.

By our actions, our words, our responses to circumstances, and our joy during those circumstances, we represent Jesus to our part of the world.

How does it make you feel knowing that God has chosen you to represent His name?

Ask Him today to give you discipline, strength, and passion to lift up His name this week.

DAY 3

Yes, it's the same Scripture as yesterday. Why? It includes the second part of John's mission—and yours: to call people to repentance. The word repent means "to turn away from." Basically, it's when a person understands who Jesus Christ is, turns away from the life he's been living (without Jesus as Lord), and turns to Jesus for forgiveness and Lordship (that's just a big word for being "boss").

Now, I'd guess that what John said in verses 7 and 8 didn't exactly win him many friends, but it was true. True repentance produces a life change. God doesn't promise that the friends with whom we share Christ will appreciate it. Even so, it's our mission to share Jesus. (It's God's job to lead people to Him.)

Ask God to open your eyes to the need for Jesus in the lives of your friends who don't know Him.

If you haven't accepted Jesus, how might your life change if you did?

If you've given your life to Christ, what changes have you noticed? Find a friend who knows you well (or you may want to approach a parent) and ask this person what changes she's seen in you since you decided to follow Christ. Write down her answers.

DAY 4

Luke 3:10–16

After repenting and being baptized, the people asked John, "What do we do now?" John's response was very specific. He basically said, "Live your lives in ways that bring honor to God. Learn to be content with the life God has given you—find your fulfillment in Him because everything else will pass away." This is a day for you to get personal with God. Are you ready?

Ask God to show you specific areas of your life in which you're not honoring Him. Spend a few moments giving those areas to Him.

Now, make a conscious choice not to do these activities any more—and ask God to help you. According to 1 Corinthians 10:13, you have the power to say "no" through Christ.

Find a prayer partner you trust. Ask him to pray for you in your areas of sin. Pray for him as well. The next time you feel tempted to sin in these areas, stop and pray for your prayer partner and yourself.

DAY 5

James 4:13-14

Why is your mission so important? Because life goes by so fast. It really is like a vapor. Seventy years ago students like you were at camps, church services, revivals, or prayer meetings—just like you are now. They were making choices about where to find their security. Now, for most of them, their lives are either over or nearing their end.

From generation to generation, God calls students like you and asks if you'll be willing to stand up for Him in your generation. Read Psalm 103:13-18. God knows your life is like a vapor, yet He still says, "Hey, follow me! I know what's best for you. I made you, remember?" How exciting to know that every morning when you wake up, the living God is leading your life.

How do you know God loves you?

What's keeping you from knowing God or from becoming all that God wants you to be?

Take some time and respond to God about what He's teaching you.

HIS BAPTISM

MEMORY VERSE:

"Those who accepted his message were baptized, and about three thousand were added to their number that day." (Acts 2:41)

INTRODUCTION

The exciting thing about the life of Christ is that He didn't just die for our sins; He also showed us how to live. This week we'll look at Jesus' first recorded public act of obedience—being baptized by John the Baptist. That's what I love about Jesus: He modeled what He taught. Jesus wants you to trust Him and to build your life around what will last.

You may ask, "But what about other things in life? They last, too." Let's take money and popularity, for instance—just two of the things many people build their lives around. I've read story after story about lottery winners who were totally broke within a few years of winning because of their liberal spending and their many loans to friends and family members who never repaid them. And even those winners who keep their money often live sad, empty lives—still wanting more but realizing "more" doesn't make them happier.

Also consider a life based on popularity. Even if you're popular now, that's certainly no guarantee that you'll have a life of success. Many people who are popular during their school years get out into the real world and discover they're just like everyone else. This doesn't mean you should try to avoid being popular or friendly, but it does mean you mustn't base your life on how others feel about you.

Don't seek to live a life based on things that aren't really worthwhile. As you begin another week, ask God to give you the wisdom to see life from His eternal perspective.

DAY 1
Matthew 3:13-17

I love Jesus' response to John's question about being baptized.
Jesus basically said, "Let it be done now! It is right and fulfills
what I am to do." Jesus didn't wait until He felt like it was time.
He immediately obeyed God's desire for His life—to be publicly
baptized. What an example to us! When we learn a truth or a
command of God, we're to obey—without delay. The result was that
God said in verse 17, "This is my Son, whom I love; with Him I am
well pleased." Each time you obey God—beginning with becoming
a Christian and being baptized—it also pleases Him. It's so hard to
grasp that we can actually make God happy. Learning to live life
based upon trust in God and obedience to His Word—rather than
how we feel—is critical to pleasing God.

So far in your journey, what do you love or appreciate the most
about Jesus?

Stop now and thank Jesus for this characteristic that you appreciate.
Also thank Him for loving you and for showing you how life is to
be lived.

DAY 2

Romans 6:3-4

Why is baptism so important, especially since it doesn't save a person?

What is baptism?

- It's your first act of obedience to God after becoming a Christian. Remember that baptism always follows salvation, not the other way around.
- It's God's choice for you to publicly profess your faith in Jesus to others.
- It's an act of identifying yourself with Jesus and His Lordship.
- It's symbolic of dying to your old self (going down into the water) and beginning a new life with Jesus as your Lord (rising out of the water).

Why was it important that Jesus be baptized?

What's God teaching you today through this portion of Scripture?

DAY 3
Acts 2:41

Jesus' baptism marked the beginning of His public ministry. In the same way, when you're baptized as an act of obedience, God tends to energize your life for His public use. Whenever we obey God, He honors our obedience by allowing us more opportunities to represent Him to the world. God expects us to be faithful in what He asks or gives us to do (Matthew 25:23). Then we're allowed to share in His joy—a joy that goes far beyond our circumstances.

Instead of your IQ (intelligence quotient), how is your OQ (obedience quotient)?

If you're a Christian, and you've been baptized, write down the date of your baptism and who baptized you.

If you're a Christian but haven't followed God's command to be baptized, why haven't you completed this first act of obedience?

DAY 4

John 1:29-34

This is a great passage of Scripture that shares the possible results of obeying God in every area of your life, but specifically in the area of baptism. John revealed in verse 31 that he baptized in order that Jesus might be revealed to the people of Israel. He also stated in verse 34 that after baptizing Jesus, he testified that Jesus was the Son of God. One result of your public baptism is to reveal who Jesus is to others and to testify that He's the Son of God. What an exciting result of our obedience!

Although you may never know the results until you stand before God in heaven, how does it make you feel to know God used your baptism—or will use your baptism—to testify to others that Jesus is the Son of God?

From this time on, whenever you attend a baptism, ask God to use it to reveal Jesus to those who are watching. Thank Him that He'll do what He says.

DAY 5

The aspect of Jesus' baptism that fascinates me is that it pleased God. In the above passage, God revealed His pleasure while Jesus was praying. Since you're seven weeks into your journey to know Jesus Christ better, let's close out this week with some personal time with God.

Psalm 46:10-11 asks us to be still and know that He is God. God said, "Stop and realize that I am God. I am with you." Guess what that means? God is next to you—in fact, He's in you—at this very moment.

How do you feel knowing that the presence of the almighty God is always with you and will never leave you?

Ask God to allow you to enjoy His presence and to speak to you. Take five minutes to be totally still and silent. Just enjoy the presence of God. Write down any thoughts before you leave.

HIS VICTORY OVER TEMPTATION

MEMORY VERSE:

"All Scripture is God-breathed and is useful for teaching, rebuking, correcting and training in righteousness, so that the servant of God may be thoroughly equipped for every good work." (2 Timothy 3:16-17)

INTRODUCTION

Welcome to the eighth week of your journey with Jesus. This week we'll get really personal as we look at temptation: what it is, what its sources are, where our strength to fight it comes from, and how Jesus responded to it.

Sometimes temptation takes a huge form and attempts to crush us. Most often, however, temptation enters our lives in small, seemingly insignificant ways. Over time the temptation keeps knocking at the door until it eventually causes sin, negative consequences, and sometimes even total destruction.

But how would we define temptation? It's best described as "being enticed to do what is displeasing to God by a desire for personal pleasure." Another way to look at temptation is that it's a shortcut to doing something God's way. Satan usually presents his best before God brings His best. Thus we're enticed to take what looks good but is actually meant to hurt us. Thank God that as Christians we don't have to choose the shortcut. We can wait for the best.

Usually temptation begins in private but grows into public sin if it isn't dealt with. As you look into the life of Jesus Christ, ask God to prepare you to face temptation with responses similar to His.

1 Corinthians 10:11-13

How good are you at obeying warning signs? "School Zone 20 MPH," "Slow—Ice on Bridge," and "Overexposure to the sun may cause skin cancer," are just a few.

In today's Scripture passage, Paul gave us some warnings about temptation. He reminded us that we'll face temptations, but God will always provide a way of escape. The problem is that many Christians will continue to follow their feelings. In doing so they'll suffer the consequences of their choices.

What's the toughest temptation you consistently face?

How do you feel knowing that God always provides a way of escape?

Ask God to remind you that He'll provide a way of escape the next time you're tempted. Make a commitment to avoid places that tempt you.

DAY 2

Luke 4:1-13

For 40 days Jesus was alone in the desert and had no food. While He was at His lowest point both physically and mentally, Satan came after Him and tempted Him in three ways. First, Satan appealed to Jesus' physical needs. He tempted Jesus to use His power to meet His immediate need for food instead of relying upon the Father. Second, Satan tempted Jesus with everything the world had to give—power, honor, prestige, and wealth. Third, Satan appealed to Jesus' pride (the same sin Satan couldn't resist, by the way).

Jesus used two things to combat Satan's temptations. First, He used His knowledge of Scripture, and second, His trust of God. Verse 13 is key: Jesus took the way of escape. Satan did leave Jesus alone then, but only for a while as he waited for another opportunity to tempt Him.

Are you consistent in learning God's Word? It's your sword for your personal battle with temptation.

Which of the three areas of Jesus' temptation is your weakest? Write it down. Spend some time telling God where you're weak and commit to take His way of escape.

Share with your prayer partner what you've learned today.

DAY 3

1 Corinthians 10:13; James 1:13-15

Because you're a believer, Satan doesn't have free rein over your life as he does over the lives of those who aren't Christians. James and Paul taught us three important truths. First, in James 1:13 we learn the source of our temptations is Satan. Verses 14 and 15 reveal that Satan uses our own evil desires to entice us to want the things that displease God. Second, if we give in to our desires, then we participate in the sin. The third truth should sound familiar: God will always provide a way of escape.

Curiosity leads to enticement, which leads to planning to sin, which leads to sinning, which leads to continual sin, which leads to destruction. Choose God's way at the beginning: Don't give in to the temptation.

What will you do the next time you're tempted?

How will you do it?

Why will you do it?

DAY 4

Matthew 6:13; Hebrews 2:18

In Matthew 6:13, Jesus tells us how to pray concerning temptation. My pastor shared with me that God may answer this prayer in one of three ways:

- He may directly intervene through a specific way, such as a godly friend dropping by or calling you.

- He may give you good sense. For instance, your sense may tell you to turn off the computer or TV, avoid a certain party or movie, or throw away a magazine.

- He may give you supernatural inner strength to say "no." Read Hebrews 2:18 again. Some of the tools God uses in this area are prayer, the Word of God, and godly friends. Use your tools and look for God's way of escape.

In which of the three ways has God answered your prayers?

DAY 5
Romans 8:5; Jude 1:24

As we conclude our study of temptation, never forget this very important fact: God is able to keep you from falling if you'll only choose to obey Him. Read that sentence again.

In times of temptation, remember what He's taught you this week:

- He's able to keep you from falling.
- Temptation is limited in its power against Christians; it never exceeds your strength to resist it.
- Although temptation will come, God is faithful if you turn to Him.
- When temptations come, God always provides an exit.
- It's your choice to choose God's exit.
- God's way of escape may be through prayer, His Word, friends, or the good sense to flee the temptation.

What has God taught you this week about temptation? Write it down.

Once more, write down the name of your prayer partner—a godly friend you can trust with your prayer needs.

Pray that God will keep your partner from falling as well.

HE CALLED HIS DISCIPLES

MEMORY VERSE:

"'Come, follow me,' Jesus said, 'and I will send you out to fish for people.'"
(Matthew 4:19)

INTRODUCTION

Can you believe it? You're entering your ninth week of looking into the Scriptures to know Jesus in deeper ways.

A lot of people call on you to do a variety of things:

- Parents tell you to come home by curfew, clean your room, chew with your mouth closed, watch who you hang out with, and pick up your clothes.
- Teachers tell you to listen in class, do homework, follow the school dress code, do your best on tests, turn in your projects, and not snore in class.
- Friends want you to spend time with them, listen to their problems, do what they want, and drive them places.
- And many others, including boyfriends or girlfriends, employers, coaches—even the media—ask you to do things.

The most important call on your life is from God—through Jesus. This call can sometimes be drowned out as we let other voices lead us. God's call on your life will continue to gnaw at you—especially in the quiet moments— until you yield to it. Nothing else will fully satisfy you because you were wired to respond to God's call.

When you fully yield to it, you begin to discover why you have the gifts, desires, personality, and physical qualities you have. Ask God to soften your heart as we look at Jesus' call on your life.

DAY 1
Matthew 4:18–22

This week we'll look at a variety of people Jesus called. In one sense, Jesus' call was the same to Peter, Andrew, James, and John as it is to you and me. It's the call to follow Him. Here's an important truth related to today's Scripture passage. We'll study more tomorrow.

Truth #1: Jesus approached Peter, Andrew, James, and John at inconvenient times. Two of them were fishing and two were preparing nets with their father. Jesus called them to leave what they were doing and follow Him. Imagine what went through their minds: Does He mean right now? What will our families say? Do we just quit our jobs? How will we support our families? All difficult questions for sure.

Has God ever called you to do something at an awkward time? When?

Are you ready to follow Jesus at any time to any place? Why or why not?

DAY 2
Matthew 4:18-22

Today, let's read the same passage of Scripture and learn some more truths from it.

Truth #2: Jesus promised the fishermen they'd fish for people. What a great trade: to exchange fishing for fish (which are temporary) for fishing for people (whose souls are eternal). God knows what really satisfies us.

Truth #3: Peter, Andrew, James, and John responded to Jesus' call immediately. They didn't think about it or discuss it. They simply obeyed at once.

God also wants you to respond to His call with immediate obedience—in all areas of your life. To delay following Him could have devastating consequences for your life's purpose.

Is there an area in which you've delayed following God? What could be a negative consequence if you continue to delay? Talk to God about this.

DAY 3
Mark 10:17-23

Jesus wants you to trust Him in every area of your life, from dating to academics. Today you read about the response of the rich young ruler. This young man valued material possessions over Jesus. Even though Jesus loved him (v. 21), He let the young man walk away. Jesus never forces you to follow Him.

Is there anything in your life that hinders you from following Christ (such as a relationship, a sport, grades, a job, money)?

If the answer is yes, then that area has priority over Jesus. That's a tough statement, but it's true. Jesus wants you to follow Him first. Everything else in your life is temporal—it can be taken away from you immediately. Do all things to the best of your ability, but build your life around your relationship with Jesus.

DAY 4

Matthew 9:9-13

I love this passage! Jesus called Matthew, a hated tax collector, to follow Him. Matthew did so immediately. Then he threw a party. He invited all his friends to come meet Jesus.

Following Jesus is the only way to live life fully without shame and regret. Some people believe the Christian life is boring. Not so! When some boring "religious people" complained about the "sinners" at Matthew's party, Jesus told them He came for people who needed Him—the sick and the sinful.

Write down the names of some "spiritually sick" people you could introduce to Jesus by inviting them to church.

What church events would they relate to the most?

Start praying for them. Start inviting them.

DAY 5

Jonah 1:1-3

Let's look at one more person's response to the call of God—Jonah. How did he respond? He said "no" and then he ran away. Imagine that—he tried to run away from God. Where could he go? Psalm 139:7-12 says there is nowhere you can go that God is not there already. Yet Jonah told God "no," ran to another city, bought a ticket on a boat, and fled. After much "whaling" and bellyaching, Jonah eventually made a choice to follow God.

How silly we can be in trying to run from God. Like Jonah, we only end up hurting ourselves. And when we finally stop running, we discover (to our amazement) that God is right beside us saying, "Are you ready to trust Me?"

Are you a runner or an obeyer?

Are you running from God in any area of your life right now?

Write down why you wouldn't trust God in this area since He's all-knowing, all-powerful, all-present, and absolutely loves you.

Talk to God right now about this area. Be totally honest.

Do you know someone who is running from God? Write her initials here and pray for God to do whatever it takes to bring this person back to Him.

HIS FIRST MIRACLE

MEMORY VERSE:

"What Jesus did here in Cana of Galilee was the first of the signs through which he revealed his glory; and his disciples believed in him." (John 2:11)

INTRODUCTION

This week we'll take another look at God as He lived among us in the flesh—Jesus Christ. Jesus is amazing; therefore, studying His life brings out amazing truths that cause one to fall more in love with Him. The result of knowing more about Jesus and loving Him more is trust. We trust Him more because we know Him more.

We'll look at Jesus' very first public miracle—performed at a wedding feast. How appropriate! Out of all the symbols God uses to represent His relationship with us, marriage is the example used most frequently. Jesus calls Himself the bridegroom and us His bride. The interesting thing about this metaphor is the groom pursues the bride; he asks her to marry him. But unlike the traditional wedding vows, there's no "till death do us part" in our marriage to Jesus. We just go from this life to eternal life with Him.

Our journey this week will help us discover some answers to questions that most of us ask at one time or another. Questions such as "How do I know God cares about the little things in my life?" Most Christians know God is concerned about the big things like forgiveness, salvation, and worship. But does He really care about little things like whether or not we date, how we spend our free time, and what classes we take at school? These aren't earth-shattering decisions, but they're still important things to the average person.

Put on your hiking boots because we're going to continue the journey of knowing Jesus.

DAY 1

John 2:1-4

Weddings were a big event in first-century Palestine. The feast often continued for days. But if the wine ran out, then it was a huge embarrassment to the wedding host. Jesus' mother, understanding the situation, asked Jesus to intervene. Even though His time had not yet come to fully expose who He was, He honored His mother and met the needs of the wedding host.

You'd think Jesus would choose an amazing act for His first public miracle—like raising a dead person. But His first public miracle was simple: He met the need of a wedding host who wasn't even named in Scripture. His actions showed us that God is aware of our little needs and is concerned enough to get involved in them. You can feel confident in taking your needs to the Father.

What are your needs this week?

God cares about your life and all that's going on with you. Talk to Him about what's happening in your life right now. Thank Him that He's concerned about the details in your life.

DAY 2

Psalm 105:4–5; John 2:5

What Mary, the mother of Jesus, said to the servants 2,000 years ago is a good word for you: "Do whatever He tells you." When you take your needs to God and spend time with Him, your response should be obedience to whatever He reveals to you through His Word.

Sometimes God will take you out of a bad situation and sometimes He'll leave you in the situation and walk with you through it. Some people get bitter at God for leaving them in a hurtful situation. Yet God may be trying to teach them a valuable lesson: He's sufficient for all their needs.

Even though your circumstances may change, God doesn't. Learn to enjoy His fellowship in both the good times and the bad. As the psalmist said, "Look to the Lord and his strength; seek his face always. Remember the wonders he has done."

If you're ready, then tell God you're willing to obey Him and do whatever He asks, regardless of your situation.

DAY 3

John 2:7-10

Did you understand what you just read? When you obey Jesus, you'll have the best life possible, not a boring life. It's amazing how many students are afraid that if they really follow Jesus, then they'll "miss out" on life. Actually, just the opposite is true.

Why do we get the idea that Jesus wants to cheat us? (It's the devil who wants to cheat us.) Obedience brings the best life possible—life the way you're meant to live—not a meaningless, wasted life. When the servants did as Jesus commanded, He turned ordinary water into the finest wine. He'll do the same in your life—if you allow Him to. God allows you that choice because He loves you. He desires for you to choose to know and obey Him.

Why are some people afraid that following God will make them miss out on life?

Tell God why obeying Him is the way to the richest life possible… or why it isn't.

DAY 4

John 2:11

This is another eye-popping verse. This simple miracle had awesome results. Believe it or not, after Jesus made the water into wine, the disciples put their faith in Him—for the first time. It makes me wonder why they were following Him before.

I guess they were a lot like us. We go to church, and we follow Christ initially because our friends do, it seems cool, it's different or new, we feel accepted, we want to make a difference in the world, or we just want a fresh start. But then we realize who Jesus really is, and we truly put our faith in Him. That's when the real adventure begins. This is what happened to the disciples after Jesus' first miracle. Their real adventure began.

Honestly, where is your faith right now: in your friends, youth minister, pastor, the church, youth program, or Jesus? Why?

Talk to God about putting your faith in Him—and Him alone.

DAY 5

Hebrews 4:14-16

Through the life of Jesus, we must take our needs to God and trust Him to meet them in the way He chooses. Today's Scripture passage challenges you to approach God with confidence in your time of need. What does He promise to do? He may not take you out of your problem immediately, but He'll always give you grace and mercy in your time of need. In other words, He'll give you what you need and when you need it in order to walk through any situation you face. And it's impossible for Him to let you down.

Go to Him confidently and trust Him. He understands, He cares, and He's been there. Remember, every failure, every sin, and every hurt was put on Jesus at the cross.

What have you learned about Jesus this week? How can you apply it to your life?

NICODEMUS' QUESTIONS

MEMORY VERSE:

"For God so loved the world that he gave his one and only Son, that whoever believes in him shall not perish but have eternal life." (John 3:16)

INTRODUCTION

Imagine what it would be like to sit alone with Jesus and ask Him anything your heart desired to ask. Imagine He'd answer any question. What would you ask?

- Whom will I marry?
- When and how will I die?
- What college will I attend?
- What will be my major?
- What will be my job?
- What is heaven like?
- What stocks should I invest in?

Wouldn't it be something to sit down with Jesus for a while and just ask Him questions?

Our journey will now take us to a moment when someone sat alone with Jesus and asked Him a question. Although you may never hear anyone ask this, I assure you it goes through everyone's mind at some point in their lives. It can also dominate the thoughts of those who don't know Jesus: *How does one go to heaven?*

All other religions require you to earn your way to heaven, yet they also teach that you never know for sure whether you'll get there—until you die. Jesus said we could never earn a trip to heaven or be good enough to attain it.

This week we get to listen in as one man asks Jesus the question on everyone's mind: *How does one go to heaven?*

DAY 1

John 3:1-3

The Pharisees were divided about who they thought Jesus was. Some believed Jesus was the Messiah, but most did not. However, one Pharisee, Nicodemus, went to Jesus to get some answers. Apparently, Nicodemus wanted to talk to Jesus in private because he approached Him during the night. He must have feared the other Pharisees would persecute him or laugh at him.

Nicodemus started off by showing his respect for Jesus by using the honorable title of "Rabbi," and by admitting that God was working through Him. But Jesus already knew Nicodemus' heart and what he wanted to ask. That's Jesus—He knows our hearts. Therefore, we can approach Him with honesty and openness.

Look back at verse 3. Jesus answered Nicodemus' question before he even asked it. Nicodemus was going to ask the question on everyone's mind: *How does one go to heaven?* And Jesus' response was, "I tell you the truth, no one can see the kingdom of God unless he is born again." Jesus got right to the point. He will never waste your time.

What one question would you love to ask Jesus?

Some people use the phrase "born again" a lot. What does this phrase really mean?

DAY 2

John 3:4-8

A person must be born again to go to heaven. There are no exceptions. The sacrifice Jesus paid on the cross for our sins is not to be watered down. It's the only way to heaven. It's the condition that God established for salvation—a spiritual rebirth made possible by Jesus dying for our sins, and satisfying God's justice.

Nicodemus asked how it was possible to be born a second time. Jesus clarified His answer: The first birth is through water (physical birth); being born again is when a person invites Jesus into her life (spiritual birth). How do you recognize this second birth? One way is to look at the outward results of an inward change. It's similar to the wind. You cannot see the wind; you can see its effect (e.g., swaying grasses or moving branches). You can't see the Spirit of God enter someone through personal repentance, but you can see the results through the change in her life.

If you've already invited Jesus into your life and are following Him, then what are some specific ways you've seen your life change?

DAY 3
John 3:9

"How can this be?" What a great question! How can a person be changed inside?

Being changed by the new birth may seem as mysterious to you as it did to Nicodemus. How can God actually transform your life into something new? When you turn from your sin and place your trust in Christ, you become part of His family. So, why is it sometimes difficult to follow Christ? Why does God sometimes seem so far away? How can your life really be like the Bible says it's supposed to be? You may have a lot more questions about this "new birth."

Questions aren't a bad thing. Just do what Nicodemus did: Take your questions to Jesus and allow Him to provide you with answers—in His time.

In your Journal Space., write some questions you have about your faith and your walk with Christ. Then ask Jesus to help you to see His truth.

DAY 4

In spite of all Jesus has said and done, many people won't accept Him as their Savior. And many of your friends won't accept what you tell them about Jesus, either. So don't be surprised.

Even though many will reject Him, many will also accept Him. And guess what? God desires to use you and me as the messengers of His good news. If you'll use your gifts, talents, passions, personality, words, and life to continually lift up the name of Jesus Christ, then people will come to Him and find eternal life. What a great promise!

What are some ways God could use your life to lift up Jesus to those around you?

What would have to happen in your life for God to use you to lift up the name of Jesus? Ask God to help you do this.

DAY 5

John 3:16–21

How deep is God's love for us? It's so deep and so real that He gave His only Son for us. God didn't just tell us He loves us; He showed us. Some people claim God is judgmental and condemning. In today's passage, Jesus clearly stated that His purpose in coming into our world was not to condemn us but to save us. What a big difference!

Some people will love darkness more than light, and they will choose to continue doing evil instead of allowing God to free them to live life in the light of His love. How foolish this is. When people finally do come into the light (v. 21), they see how God loves them and has done all that He's done in order to bring them to Himself.

This week, God wants to use you to help someone know Jesus. Are you ready?

Talk to God about your life and your willingness to be used by Him to lift up Jesus.

HE IS THE LIVING WATER

MEMORY VERSE:

"Jesus answered, 'Everyone who drinks this water will be thirsty again, but whoever drinks the water I give them will never thirst. Indeed, the water I give them will become in them a spring of water welling up to eternal life.'" (John 4:13-14)

INTRODUCTION

The exciting thing about following Jesus is that the journey is eternal; it never ends. Plus, the journey with Jesus is always exciting! In 1 Corinthians 2:9, Paul said your ears, eyes, and mind cannot conceive the things God has prepared for you. How could you ever desire to quit following Jesus? What would be worth trading your walk with Jesus? Nothing!

This week focuses on grasping the fantastic mission God has given you: To represent Him in your part of the world. Did you know that many revivals throughout history share three distinct characteristics?

- They were started by students—either teenagers or college students.
- They always occurred after a call to prayer among that generation. Could "See You at the Pole" and other youth prayer movements be God's calling upon your generation of students?
- They always followed a call to moral purity among that generation. Could "True Love Waits" and other abstinence movements be God's call upon your generation of students?

Obviously, God has His hand on your generation. This is your wake-up call to respond to God. Ask God what He wants to do with your life. If you're courageous enough, then offer Him all that you are—all the gifts and talents you have, and those you don't have.

Throughout Scripture God used people who weren't very gifted but who were willing to yield everything to Him. Are you?

DAY 1
John 4:1-9

For a Jew, going to Samaria was like going to a bad part of town. In fact, the Jews usually walked around Samaria. Of course Jesus didn't hesitate to go right through it. He even stopped at a well where a Samaritan woman was drawing water, shocked that Jesus would talk to her.

If you're ready to be the generation God uses to bring spiritual awakening to our world, then you must be willing to go anyplace God opens the door. You need to be ready to share with a person you've never dreamed you'd share with, whether that person is on the other side of the cafeteria or on the other side of the world.

Pray for God to place on your heart two or three unlikely people at your school, in your workplace, or on your sports team to whom you can show Jesus. Write down their names.

What are some of the difficulties you'll face in representing Jesus to them? Pray about these difficulties.

DAY 2

John 4:10–15

Jesus turned a simple conversation into a chance to offer forgiveness and eternal life to the Samaritan woman. God desires the same for you. He wants to take the everyday aspects of your life and turn them into opportunities for you to tell others about His eternal life and forgiveness. How exciting is that? God wants you to live with your eyes open to opportunities. It's more than just going door-to-door to conduct a survey or participating in a mission trip. God longs for you to allow Him to use your everyday life to share Jesus with others. It's much more natural.

The first step is being willing to go out of your comfort zone to establish a relationship with those who need Him. It starts by saying hello. Be a friend first, and then God will open the door of opportunity. Remember, you have streams of living water waiting to flow out of you.

Think about the two or three people you wrote down on yesterday's journal page. What are some actions you can take to begin relationships with them?

DAY 3

John 4:16-26

As Jesus talked with this woman about eternal life, she tried to change the subject. But Jesus knew all about her—He is God, after all. How did Jesus respond to the subject change? He gently shared truth with her.

At times it's tough to share truth. Yet Jesus is the way, the truth, and the life; and no one can come to the Father except through Him (John 14:6). A doctor is never afraid to share with you what treatment you need to cure an illness. Just think how much more important it is to share eternal life with someone.

Think about the people whose names you wrote earlier this week. What signs can you see that they need Jesus?

Tell God you're ready to step out in faith. Ask Him to prepare their hearts and open the door of opportunity.

DAY 4

John 4:27–38

Why were the disciples so shocked that Jesus was talking to the woman? She was a Samaritan (to whom Jews did not talk), and she was a woman (to whom men did not speak in public). Jesus ignored cultural norms to reach someone who needed Him. Shouldn't we do the same?

The Samaritan woman was so moved after her conversation with Jesus that she told others about Him. She was so enthusiastic that people came out from the town to meet Jesus. As you're willing to go to those outside your own circle of friends, God will expand your ministry to others. People are looking for something that will bring purpose to their lives.

Jesus tried to open the disciples' eyes to see the harvest—people hungering for truth—all around them. He also wants to open your eyes to see the people around you in the same way He sees them: People searching for meaning.

Spend a few minutes asking God to allow you to see the people you come in contact with every day through His eyes.

DAY 5

John 4:39–42

Many Samaritans (lonely, unloved people) came to know Jesus because He stopped long enough to talk to a lonely, hurting woman. What will happen if you befriend people outside your circle of friends? Others will come to you with questions about life. The final result is found in verse 42—they'll come to know Jesus, and not just because of your words.

Lighthouses don't fire guns or ring bells to call attention to their light; they just shine. So what are you waiting for? Go shine and let God bring about the results.

Remember praying about opportunities two days ago? Well, step out, look for the opportunities, and then write about the results. Be patient, keep building relationships, and keep sharing the truth.

WEEK 13
HIS POWER OVER NATURE

MEMORY VERSE:

"Do not be anxious about anything, but in every situation, by prayer and petition, with thanksgiving, present your requests to God. And the peace of God, which transcends all understanding, will guard your hearts and your minds in Christ Jesus." (Philippians 4:6-7)

INTRODUCTION

Storms are just a part of life. It doesn't matter where you live; eventually a storm will blow over that area. It may be a rainstorm, a thunderstorm, a sandstorm, a snowstorm, a hailstorm, a hurricane, a tornado, or a typhoon, but a storm will come. But storms blow over—they come and they go. They may come at inconvenient times, but they still eventually go. It's the same way with the storms of life. They'll come and go as well; they're just a part of living in a fallen world. We can't control the storms; we can control only our responses to them.

When difficulties come, don't panic and run. Stay with Jesus. His power will be sufficient.

DAY 1

Mark 4:35–37

Did you catch how this passage is a perfect example of storms coming into our lives? Three vital truths stand out. First, storms can come up suddenly. Our lives may be going along all right when our world suddenly caves in with no warning. Second, difficulties can threaten to swamp us just like the disciples' boat. The waves of our storm keep washing over us until we feel we're about to go under. Third, no matter how tough it is, we're not alone. Others either have gone or are going through similar problems. Verse 36 says there were also "other boats with Him." Remember, life's storms can come suddenly, but you're not alone.

Has a difficulty suddenly come into your life? If so, talk to God about it. Ask God to lead you to another Christian with whom you can talk about the crisis you're facing.

If you have no difficulties at this moment, then thank God for allowing you to have a peaceful time right now.

Mark 4:38

"Don't you care, God? Come on, where are you? Why aren't you helping me?" This is very similar to what the disciples were saying to Jesus. The storm had hit, Jesus was sleeping in the boat, and the disciples were terrified. Sometimes I wonder if Jesus had one eye open to watch how the disciples would respond to this new "test" in their lives.

The main part of the disciples' question was, "Do you care?" When storms sweep into our lives and threaten to overwhelm us, we tend to question God's love for us. We may think, *If God really loved me, why would He allow this to happen?* Instead of yielding to fear, we should depend on God more and allow Him to work in our lives through the storms.

Why does God allow difficulties to come into our lives?

Why do we tend to question God's love for us when those difficulties come?

Ask God to teach you how to trust Him and rest in Him when storms blow through your life.

DAY 3
Mark 4:39–41

This portion of Scripture is awesome. Jesus just stood up and rebuked (sharply criticized) the wind. Then He said (not yelled, shouted, or screamed), "Quiet! Be still!" At once, the storm stopped and all was calm. Wow! He criticized the wind; and with the power of His words, He calmed the storm. That's the power of our God.

But the sweet part comes next. He asked the disciples why they were afraid and why they still had no faith. After all they knew about Jesus, they still failed this test. He wanted them to know Him so well that when storms appeared, they'd trust in Him as the storm blew over.

When the reality of who Jesus was washed over their minds, the disciples were terrified because they knew they were in the presence of God in physical form. However, Jesus desires that we realize who He is and love and trust Him more.

What is some of the evidence that helps you realize Jesus is God in the flesh?

How will the information or evidence you have about Jesus cause you to trust Him and rest in Him when storms of life come?

DAY 4

Philippians 4:6-7

Paul's words about facing difficulties expressed the same truths Jesus taught. After all, Paul experienced a lot of tough things in his life, and these two verses offer some great advice for us.

The word anxious means "brooding fear." It refers to a fear that lingers on our minds and leads us to continually worry. Paul challenges us to take our difficulties to God, being thankful that God will help us. God may not take us out of our problem, but He'll help us walk through it. The result is a peace that goes beyond understanding. This peace, based on trust in God, will protect your heart and mind from worry.

What is God saying to you about storms?

DAY 5

Hebrews 4:14–16

It's so easy to get angry with God when He doesn't take away a problem—when He doesn't make the storms in our lives go away. What exactly has God promised us when storms blow into our lives? Today's Scripture passage is God's answer. God reminds us that Jesus has gone through all we go through, and He did so without sinning. Jesus understands and sympathizes with us.

God then challenges us to come boldly to Him in our time of need. If we go to Him, then He promises to give us mercy and grace to sustain us in our time of need. He doesn't promise He'll take us out of the problem, but He does promise to give us what we need to walk through it.

Write your action plan for the next time storms blow into your life.

Talk to God about what you've learned in His Word this week.

WEEK 14

BEING SALT AND LIGHT

MEMORY VERSE:

"In the same way, let your light shine before others, that they may see your good deeds and glorify your Father in heaven." (Matthew 5:16)

INTRODUCTION

It has been said that there are three kinds of people in the world:

1. Those few who make things happen.
2. The many who watch things happen.
3. The overwhelming majority who have no idea what's happening.

I don't know about you, but since I have only one life to live, I want to live a life that makes a difference. God designed us with a desire to live a life that matters. That's why the search for meaning and love in life is so powerful. Some people are willing to go to extremes to find love or meaning.

This search for meaning brings us to the next stage in our journey in developing a relationship with Jesus. By developing a dynamic relationship with Him, we can live a life that's exciting, meaningful, fulfilling—and way above the norm.

If you buy a new car, a new game system, or a new computer, don't you want to know how to get the most out of it—to understand all of its functions and how to use it most effectively? Usually you'll accomplish this by reading the owner's manual or having someone teach you how to use the item.

Basically, that's what you'll encounter for the next two weeks—Jesus' instructions on how to live life to the fullest. Jesus gave us clear directions on living life. But there's one catch—the power and authority to live life by these principles comes only from God and only when you choose to become a Christian.

So are you ready? If so, let's take a look at how to live life according to the very Author of life.

DAY 1

Matthew 5:1-5

The first 12 verses of Jesus' Sermon on the Mount are called the "Beatitudes." Let's look at the first three today.

Verse 3: "Poor in spirit" is another way of saying, "I'm nothing on my own. I have needs I can't meet." When you realize this, your heart becomes pliable to God, and He can change you. And once He does, you inherit "the kingdom of heaven."

Verse 4: When you realize you can't change others—much less yourself—you mourn. God then comforts you with, "I am here; I am enough for you."

Verse 5: The thought of your inadequacy drives you to God. He responds, "Okay, now you're ready to 'inherit the earth'; you'll represent my name to others." At this point, life can become very fulfilling.

Which beatitude speaks most to you?

What will you do with this knowledge?

DAY 2

Matthew 5:6-8

The first three beatitudes show us how badly we need God. We need His forgiveness, wisdom, strength, and guidance. Once we realize this, the next three principles begin to flow into reality.

Verse 6: When you're humble (or meek, v. 5), you'll develop a deep hunger to know God and become what He wants you to be. When you're hungry for God, He fills you with Himself. Being filled with God is the only way to satisfy your deepest needs.

Verse 7: Because we hunger for God (His righteousness, v. 6), we become more understanding (merciful) of others' faults. We begin to show compassion to friends, family members, and others. This mercy is then returned to us.

Verse 8: Then God begins to give us a pure heart, which allows us to "see" Him. In other words, we're better able to see life as God does and to hear His voice. Obedience becomes more natural. We grasp that it's about God, not about us.

How serious are you about knowing Jesus?

Ask God to give you a deep hunger to know Him and become what He wants you to be. Begin to put yourself in places and around people whom God can use to feed this new hunger.

DAY 3

Matthew 5:9-12

The last three beatitudes flow from the first six, although they also lead to fulfillment. The final two are pretty tough.

Verse 9: The first six beatitudes lead you to become a "peacemaker"—one who brings peace to others and between others. People will begin to see you as one who carries the name of God wherever you go. People will be drawn to Jesus by your life.

Verse 10: Your obedience to God makes Satan angry. You'll experience spiritual warfare. Some people—maybe even your friends—will persecute (harass) you. God says not to worry; He's in control, and His entire kingdom is behind you.

Verses 11-12: Even if people insult you and tell lies about you, rejoice! Why? Because your reward will be great. You'll also set a great example for others.

What fears do you have about standing for Jesus? Talk to God about them.

Do you want to become a person after God's heart—someone who will do everything God wants you to do? (God described King David this way; see Acts 13:22.) Why or why not?

DAY 4

Matthew 5:13–16

The Beatitudes lead you to make a difference. It's not that God wants you to become the salt of the earth or the light of the world. In the moment you become a Christian, you're already the salt of the earth and the light of the world.

It's true salt can lose its flavor (its impact) and light can be hidden. The same is true for you. God wants to use your life to flavor (bring real life to) others and to preserve (fulfill) their lives to be used by God. As people see your good deeds, they'll know it's from God.

How are you doing as salt and light? Write down a few specific ways God has used you as salt or light or ways He could use you if you were willing.

Ask God to give you opportunities to be salt and light to others this week. Record what God does.

DAY 5
Matthew 5:43-48

It's easy to love those who love us. Jesus says the real test is how
we respond to our enemies—those who don't treat us with love.
How did Jesus respond to those who hated Him? I seem to
remember He died for them. He didn't say you had to like what
your enemies do, but you are called to love them and pray for
them. You love by your actions. If you're thinking that it's not normal
to love your enemies, then remember, God always gives
His followers the power to live above the norm.

Do you have any enemies—people who don't show love to you?

What is one loving action you could do for them this week?
Commit to this action and commit to pray for them each day.
Record their responses after you've shown love to them.

SEEK FIRST HIS KINGDOM

MEMORY VERSE:

"Can any one of you by worrying add a single hour to your life?" (Matthew 6:27)

INTRODUCTION

At times, Jesus' teaching can be difficult to follow. His teachings are usually the opposite of what our culture believes is right. They're also a radical departure from what most people choose to do. To be honest, it's only through the power of Jesus Christ living inside you that you're able to follow Him and His teachings day to day. If you choose to totally follow Him, then the results are life changing, exciting, and eternal. He is not a boring God.

Our adventure of following Jesus takes us to Matthew 6 and 7 this week. These chapters are full of great teachings on how to live. Because our time limits what we can look at, I challenge you to go back over Matthew 6 and 7 at a later date and look at all the great things Jesus has to tell you.

It's so important for you to spend time in God's Word each day. You'll never become what God made you to be just by hearing others talk about God's Word on Sundays and Wednesdays or during camps and retreats. That would be like eating meals only on those days.

God desires for you to take a personal plunge into His Word. He wants to teach you what you need to know as you dig into the truths of the Bible. God will use His Word to—

- Uncover things in life that will harm you.
- Show you glimpses of who He is so you'll love and trust Him more.
- Give you direction on how to live a real life.
- Encourage you when life gets tough.

Don't miss the adventure!

DAY 1

Matthew 6:19-21

Jesus jumped right into what controls most of us. Was He criticizing us for valuing money, CDs, computers, relationships, sports, bands, and skateboards? No! Look again at verses 19-21. He said your heart, mind, and actions will center on what you value most.

Jesus wants you to value your relationship with Him and your obedience to Him more than any other "treasure." Why? Because everything else—your health, family, money, trophies, relationships, and looks, to name a few—can be taken away. It's okay to enjoy those things but don't hold them too tightly. Seek first your relationship with Jesus. It will last for eternity.

Most Christians agree with the latter truths, but few live as though they do. Write down five things you value the most and how much time you spend on them in a week.

Now write how much time you spend on your relationship with Jesus. Surprised? Talk to God about this today.

DAY 2

Matthew 6:22-24

This teaching of Jesus can really hit home. He said to be careful—to guard—what you allow into your mind and life. Many times we wonder, *Why am I struggling in this area?* or *Why am I having these thoughts?* or *Why do I do what I do?* The reason is we let things into our lives that cloud our ability to hear and see Jesus.

Let's get practical for a moment. Be careful what you allow into your mind. For instance, choose not to open that pornographic website. Choose not to see movies or listen to music that open your heart and mind to what displeases God. Choose wisely whom you date. Choose carefully where you go and with whom you go. Remember, you can't be tempted by what you don't know. In other words, avoid things that you know may tempt you. Guard your heart. Guard your mind. Guard your life.

Let's get honest with God. What things are you exposing yourself (God's temple) to that are dragging you down?

Tell God your struggles and sincerely ask for—and then take—His way of escape.

DAY 3

Matthew 6:25-27

Don't worry. It's easy for God to say, but it's much harder for us to live. Life can be so full of stressful moments from school to relationships to how you look with that big pimple on your nose. So why shouldn't you worry?

God gives you a great clue: Worrying won't add a single hour to your life. It adds only stress, ulcers, and possibly sinful behavior as you attempt to relieve the stress. However, verse 26 reminds you that you're of extreme value to God. He loves you deeply. Jesus taught that you should obey God, do your best (1 Corinthians 10:31), and leave the results to God. Whatever you can't change (for example, your freckles) let God have it and go on with the life He's given you. Sure, you'll probably still worry a little from time to time, but it helps a lot to know that God will take care of us.

What are some things you tend to worry about? Why?

Does your worry change anything? How could God help you in these areas?

DAY 4

Matthew 7:1-12

In these verses, Jesus gave us two very important principles for following Him. First, He told us not to judge others. The word judge means to form an opinion about someone or something. Instead, Jesus challenged us to make sure our own lives are in line with His will. It's okay to encourage and even confront others (in private) if we love them, but we aren't to sit in judgment over anyone else. In fact, verse 6 says that judging will cause some people to react with anger and harm toward the judge.

Second, Jesus said to seek Him at all times. He said we'll find our real needs are met when we take them to Him.

Have you been judging someone instead of encouraging him? Ask God to forgive you.

Then contact that person today and encourage him.

DAY 5

Matthew 7:24-29

What an awesome way for Jesus to close His sermon! (In fact, why don't you read Matthew chapters 5 through 7 again now?) Basically, Jesus said, "Okay, I've told you how to live, and I've given you the power to do it. Now live it. Don't just think it was a nice spiritual lesson. Show Me you believe Me."

Jesus said problems and difficulties will come. But if we put His words into practice, then they'll anchor us during tough times. If we don't do what He said, then life's hard times will blow our lives apart, leaving us bitter and angry.

Read verses 28-29 again. I'm also amazed at His teachings. Are you?

Of all that you've learned this week, what's the hardest thing to put into practice?

What will help you do it?

Take a few moments and talk to God about what He's taught you through His Word.

WEEK 16
THE CENTURION'S FAITH

MEMORY VERSE:

"Now faith is confidence in what we hope for and assurance about what we do not see." (Hebrews 11:1)

INTRODUCTION

I remember some amazing facts I heard during an astronomy class years ago:

- Our sun is so large that more than one million earths could fit inside it.
- The distance from the earth to the sun is 93 million miles.

- Some believe our galaxy, the Milky Way, contains more than 100 billion stars.
- There are at least 50 billion other galaxies in the universe.

Now apply this newly discovered scientific knowledge to God's Word. In 1 Kings 8:27, King Solomon said that all of the heavens could not contain God. Psalm 8:3-4 says that when we consider the majesty of the heavens, we're reminded that we are small and seemingly unimportant. Yet in Psalm 8:5-8, God continues to say that's not true. We're of extreme value to God, and He loves us deeply.

This week our adventure with Jesus will take us deeper into the area of faith. Jesus' compassion for people is amazing. However, Jesus really wanted the people He encountered to trust Him. He asks the same from us.

God's desire for you this week is that your faith in Him will mature. God calls you into a faith that will allow Him complete access to your life at all times. How exciting would it be to have God freely moving and directing your life at all times? If God has that kind of control over your life, then He'll consistently use you to draw others to Himself. He'll do it simply by the way you live your daily life.

DAY 1

Luke 7:1-9

Only twice in the New Testament is it recorded that Jesus was amazed. He was amazed by the unbelief of the people in His hometown of Nazareth (Mark 6:4-6), and He was amazed by the faith of the centurion in today's Scripture passage. So it's obvious that few things amazed Jesus, yet the faith of the centurion did.

Let's take a look at this centurion—a Roman officer in charge of 100 soldiers. (1) He had a deep love and concern for his servant. (2) He was probably not a follower of Jesus. Yet he knew enough about Jesus to trust His word without having to see Jesus in action, meaning Jesus' words were enough for Him. (3) He was humble; he knew who he was, and he knew who Jesus was.

Use this man of faith as a mirror to check your own life. Does your genuine concern for others, especially non-Christians, earn you respect from those who know you? If not, ask God to work in this area of your life.

Are you known as one who genuinely cares for your friends and is loyal to them? If not, deal with it before God right now.

Are you developing a faith in which Jesus' Word is enough to make you obey? If not, ask God to help you build your faith.

DAY 2

Luke 7:9-10

Imagine all that Jesus—as God—had seen and experienced, yet this situation amazed Him. What is faith? Webster's Dictionary says faith is "complete trust." That's God's desire for us: That we would know Him so well that we would trust Him completely. The centurion did, and it amazed Jesus. The result of his faith was that his servant was healed. An example of genuine faith was given to all of Israel—and to all who read this story in Luke 7.

What is one area of your life in which you're having a hard time trusting God this week? Tell Him about it—and tell Him why.

Ask God to speak to you through this passage of Scripture. Spend today meditating on this passage. Chew on it and apply it to your life.

DAY 3

Hebrews 11:1-6

The Bible defines *faith* as being sure (having no doubt) of what you hope for and certain of what you have not seen or cannot see. In other words, faith is trusting in the words of Jesus (God) without having to see immediate action. Remember, the centurion basically said, "Just say the word and my servant will be healed. You don't even have to physically be there. I know who you are, and I know you have authority over all." That's the definition of a mature faith.

In fact, faith is so important that the Bible says without it, you cannot please God. Those are some tough words. There is a reward for those who earnestly (intensely and seriously) seek God. If you continue to read Hebrews 11, then you'll read about many people who exercised their faith in God and discovered the results of their faith.

What's missing from your faith and preventing it from becoming a mature faith?

Talk to God about your areas of weakness. Ask Him to continue to give you opportunities to exercise and mature your faith.

THE CENTURION'S FAITH

DAY 4

Hebrews 11:32-39

The Bible is always honest about the people who've followed God. It shows their strengths and weaknesses; it explains the cost of following Him. In this passage we see that during their time on earth, some people received rewards for their faith, while others had very difficult times and received their rewards later (in heaven). We must understand that some of us will be called by God to go through very tough times. Therefore, God wants to mature our faith so we'll be better able to focus on Him during those difficult times.

What are some situations that may arise in your future that will require you to have faith in Jesus?

Is your faith ready for these situations?

Ask God to continue to prepare you to complete the mission in life that He has planned for you.

DAY 5
Psalm 8; Psalm 23

Today will be different. Ask God to speak to your heart from these two psalms. Read them again and spend a few minutes in silence thinking about these words from God.

Write down two things God tells you or reveals to you from these two psalms. If He says nothing clearly, then just enjoy a few moments in the presence of God.

How can you exercise your faith based upon what God said in Psalms 8 and 23?

JOHN THE BAPTIST'S DOUBT

MEMORY VERSE:

"The blind receive sight, the lame walk, those who have leprosy are cleansed,
the deaf hear, the dead are raised, and the good news is proclaimed to the poor."
(Matthew 11:5)

INTRODUCTION

Do you ever have doubts about the Christian life? Do you ever question
the Bible? Do you ever wonder why God allows certain things to happen?
It seems to be so easy to trust and believe when things are going well,
when there's no need to stretch our faith. But when things don't go the way
we want them to, we either doubt God or get angry at God. It's almost as
if we consider Him to be our personal Santa Claus or genie in a bottle. We
thank Him for the good things, but we also blame Him for the bad.

In actuality, tough times can result from our not living the way God
planned or from things that are completely out of our control. In either
case, God often uses adversity to shape our character. And if we're honest,
we'll admit that we tend to grow the most during our difficulties.

God compares our relationship with Him to a marriage. Every marriage
faces difficult times, but a marriage will succeed when the husband and
wife remain committed to each other in love. You must learn how to rise
above your circumstances because they're always changing. God, on the
other hand, remains constant.

Circumstances never make or break you—they just reveal who you are
deep inside. Will you praise God in both the bad and the good times—or
is He only your God when He does what you want? My desire is that you'll
learn to trust God no matter what happens in your life.

Grab your Bible and let's see what God will teach us this week.

DAY 1
Matthew 11:1-3

Doubting isn't a bad thing if it leads you to seek truth. And most people will begin a time of deep soul-searching when their faith is challenged by unexpected circumstances.

John the Baptist was chosen to "prepare the way" for Jesus. John knew Jesus (they were cousins), and he publicly proclaimed Jesus to be the Messiah. But now John doubted. Why? Herod put John in prison not only for preaching about Jesus, but also for speaking out about the evil things Herod had done. Now John feared for his life. He was probably thinking, If I'm going to lose my life over this, I want to be sure it's true. It makes sense, doesn't it? So John asked Jesus point-blank: "Are you the One...or should I look elsewhere?"

Why do you follow Jesus?

Are your heart and mind settled on the fact that Jesus is the way, the truth, and the life and that no one comes to God but through Him? Why or why not?

Talk to God today about why you really follow Him.

JOHN THE BAPTIST'S DOUBT

DAY 2

Remember John the Baptist's doubts from yesterday? Jesus' response was awesome. He told John's disciples to go back and report all that they'd heard and seen. In other words, Jesus was saying that all of the evidence confirmed beyond a shadow of a doubt that He was who He claimed to be: The Messiah.

When doubts come, look at the evidence from Jesus' life, history, archaeology, prophecies, changed lives (yours and others'), and the results of not following Jesus that can be seen around the world. The evidence is everywhere. In 1 Corinthians 15, Paul offered us the evidence that caused him to follow Jesus. Don't be afraid of your doubts; use them to dig deeper into who Jesus is. You'll wind up believing in Him more.

What's the biggest doubt you have right now?

What do you usually do when things go wrong?

What can you do to increase your faith when doubts come?

Talk honestly with God about your doubts.

DAY 3

Matthew 11:16–19

When you were a child, did you ever have a pretend wedding? The bride walked down the aisle and said "I do" to the groom. Then everyone had a party. Children in Jesus' time went to weddings and funerals, and they may have acted out those experiences during their times of play.

In today's passage, Jesus compared the people to children who wouldn't play either one of those games. John's preaching had been hard, focused on people's sinfulness and their need to repent (like a funeral). The Jews knew about his teaching, but they didn't want to be a part of his mission. They doubted John's message. Jesus, on the other hand, talked about the joy of the coming kingdom (like a wedding). They doubted Him also.

The truth is circumstances change. Sometimes you face hard truths. God is there. Sometimes life will be full of excitement. God is there, too.

How do you feel knowing that regardless of your circumstances, God doesn't change and He walks with you through all circumstances—good and bad?

Tell God how you feel today and how much you love and trust Him.

DAY 4

James 1:5–8

Doubt can be harmful when you hold it inside and don't seek answers, or when you use it as an excuse to sin. James challenged us to ask God for wisdom during times of doubt.

It's not good to hold doubt inside. Get some godly counsel from a strong Christian, search your Bible for answers, ask God to give you wisdom, and stay active in your church. How can a doctor help you if you never go to see him? Likewise, how can God help you find answers if you don't ask Him? Every doubt can be an opportunity to learn and grow.

To whom, what, or where will you go for answers when you doubt? Talk to God about this.

DAY 5

Job 1:9–11; 42:12

God's Word is full of truth if we'll only mine for this gold. The book of Job offers a different twist on doubt. In Job 1, Satan said that Job followed God only because Job's life was good. But if God allowed difficult times in Job's life, Satan argued, then Job would curse God.

Is that how we are? Do we love God only in the good times? God allowed a test to reveal the basis of Job's love. After a very difficult time, Job's faith remained solid. And as a result, God honored Job's life.

How would you hold up in a faith test?

The only statement of Jesus' that's simple enough for me to comprehend when my heart is breaking is—"Follow me." I cannot understand life because life sometimes doesn't make sense. But I can understand Jesus' words: "Follow me."

Is there anything you'd have to be sure of in order to trust God during difficult times? What?

The only thing we really need to be sure of is that we trust in God.

HE FED THE HUNGRY

MEMORY VERSE:

"Then Jesus declared, 'I am the bread of life. Whoever comes to me will never go hungry, and whoever believes in me will never be thirsty.'" (John 6:35)

INTRODUCTION

One of the most important parts of our journey with Jesus is learning to trust Him in every area of our lives. Most of us worry over so many things: *Will I pass this test? Will I ever get a boyfriend/girlfriend? What college should I attend? Can I make the team? How do I get rid of zits? Can I pass my driver's license test?* The list goes on and on. There are so many things to be concerned about that our minds can easily slip into worry and stress. God's gentle voice tells us to slow down and seek Him first. Then He'll direct our lives and meet our needs.

God knows and understands our needs. God is willing and able to meet our needs and wants us to find rest in Him, especially during the hectic times of life. Knowing God's in control brings joy and confidence to life.

A few years ago, a church in Texas asked children to write notes to God. Here are a couple of examples of what they wrote:

> *Dear God,*
> *In class they told us what you do. Who does it when you are on vacation?*

> *Dear God,*
> *Did you mean for the giraffe to look like that or was it an accident?*

What wonderfully honest questions from the mouths of children! However, God doesn't take vacations, and God doesn't make accidents. He's in control.

Let's get back on the journey and learn how to rest in God.

DAY 1
Luke 9:10–11

Jesus always modeled what He wanted His disciples to learn. That's one reason our journey with Him is so exciting. He taught with both His words and His life.

In today's passage Jesus took His disciples away for some rest and a private retreat in Bethsaida, a beautiful little town on the shores of Galilee. When the crowds heard where Jesus had gone, they followed Him. Jesus and the disciples had every right to send them away so they could rest for a few days—yet they did not. Jesus welcomed the people joyfully. He taught them about God's plan for life, and He healed those who had physical, spiritual, or mental difficulties. By His example Jesus said, "I care about your needs. I will meet your needs, and I want you to help meet the needs of others."

What is your biggest need this week?

Take your need to God right now and trust Him with it.

DAY 2
Luke 9:12-13

Jesus, the disciples, and well over 5,000 people were all in a remote area near Bethsaida for a teaching time. The afternoon was waning, and everyone was getting hungry. There were no fast-food places around, and thousands of hungry people don't make for a happy experience. The disciples were worried, and they encouraged Jesus to send the crowd away to scavenge for food on their own.

Here's where it gets interesting. Jesus said, "You go feed them." The disciples were shocked. Can't you just hear them stammering, "Us? We have only a few fish and a little bread. Who has any money on them? I don't." I believe Jesus smiled at this moment because He was about to remind them who He is.

God often lets us exhaust our attempts to meet our own needs. He reminds us that only He can really fulfill our lives. The disciples were inadequate—and so are we. We need to depend totally on God for all things—not just the things we believe we can't handle ourselves.

What are some ways you've tried to meet the needs that only God can meet?

What were the results?

Talk to God about His desire to be the One who meets all the needs in your life.

DAY 3

Luke 9:14-16

The feeding of the 5,000 is one of only two miracles of Jesus recorded in all four Gospels (Matthew, Mark, Luke, and John). The other is the resurrection of Jesus. So this miracle must have been important. Watch closely when Jesus stepped in. As soon as the disciples admitted they were inadequate, Jesus told them what to do. He met the need.

What are some of your fears about God meeting your needs?

What has God's Word taught you about meeting your needs?

DAY 4

Luke 9:17

After the disciples realized they were inadequate to meet the people's needs and obeyed Jesus' directions completely, something amazing happened. All of the people were satisfied. Not some, not most, but all were satisfied.

When we attempt to meet our own needs or the needs of others without doing it God's way, it never seems to satisfy for very long. Yet when we admit that we're inadequate, trust Jesus, and obey God's directions in His Word, it brings a satisfaction that can last us through difficult times.

But there's still more! Not only was everyone satisfied, but they also had an abundance of food left over—even more food than they started with. That's God. Trust Him to meet your needs, and He'll do more than you can imagine.

Can you think of some ways you've attempted to meet certain needs outside of God's direction? What were the results?

Commit to seek God and His direction during your times of need. Talk with Him about what you've learned this week.

DAY 5

Matthew 6:31–34; John 6:35

Jesus said some amazing things in these two Scripture passages.
Read them again—slowly—and record your thoughts in the
Journal Space.

Jesus said He's what you need to get through each day. He will take
care of you, so you don't have to worry. He knows what you need.
He challenges you to seek Him—and in return, He'll give you what
you need for each day. Non-followers of Jesus are always running
after things to find satisfaction; but God knows your needs, and
He's ready to meet them.

Why are you waiting? Quit worrying. Quit trying to meet your
own needs. Run to God and watch Him meet your needs.

Spend some time thanking God for His promise to meet your
daily needs.

HE FED THE HUNGRY

PETER'S CONFESSION

MEMORY VERSE:

"And I tell you that you are Peter, and on this rock I will build my church, and the gates of Hades will not overcome it." (Matthew 16:18)

INTRODUCTION

God's plan for you and me includes our active involvement in a local church. God never intended for us to exist alone, but planned for us to be involved in a community of believers.

Geese fly in a V formation because as each bird flaps its wings, it creates a lift for the bird immediately behind it. This gives the entire flock a much greater flying range than if each bird flew on its own. What are some ways we can compare a flock of geese to the church?

First, whenever a goose falls out of formation, it suddenly feels the resistance of going it alone and quickly gets back into formation. If we have as much sense as a goose, then we'll stay in formation with those who are following Christ instead of trying to do things our own way.

Second, when the lead goose gets tired, it rotates to the back of the formation and another goose flies in front. It pays to take turns doing hard jobs with others.

Third, the geese honk from behind to encourage those up front to keep up their speed. It's called encouragement and accountability.

Finally, when a goose gets sick or wounded, two geese fall out of formation and follow it down to protect it. They stay with the injured goose until it's either able to fly or dead. Then they launch out on their own or with another flock of geese until they catch up with their own group. If we only had the sense of a goose, then we'd care for each other in the same way.

Let's see what Jesus said about the church.

DAY 1
Matthew 16:13–20

Jesus gave His disciples a test. He asked them who they thought He was. Peter, who was the most verbal of the disciples, blurted out that Jesus was "the Messiah, the Son of the living God." Jesus then told the disciples that He would build His church on "this rock." Jesus' statement played on the meaning of Peter's name (which in Greek is *petros*; it means "rock" or "stone"). This didn't mean Jesus would literally build His church on top of Peter. It meant Peter was representative of all the disciples who started and served as leaders of the early church. (Ephesians 2:19-20 is another passage that corresponds with what Jesus said here.)

Jesus also said that the keys to the kingdom of heaven were given to the church—along with awesome power. He stated that nothing would overcome it. We can be sure Jesus will protect His church.

Are you actively involved in a church? If not, why not?

Right now, stop and pray for God to use your church to accomplish what He desires.

If you aren't enjoying the blessing of being an active member of a church, then pray that God will lead you to a church where you can join with others to build His kingdom.

DAY 2

Acts 2:42

The early church devoted itself to four characteristic actions:

> *Apostles' teaching—the early church was devoted to learning the truth of God's Word through verbal teaching.*

> *Fellowship—the early church devoted themselves to each other and cared for one another.*

> *Breaking bread—the early church ate together and held each other accountable to remember Jesus through the Lord's Supper.*

> *Prayer—the early church devoted themselves to both private and public prayer. And they didn't pray half-heartedly.*

Does your church do the kinds of things the early church did?

If not, what would your church need to do differently to be more like the early church?

DAY 3

Acts 2:43

When was the last time you were in church and felt awe because of who God is or because of what He was doing in your church? When was the last time you actually witnessed the power of God moving in your church and were filled with wonder? I'm not talking about a spiritual high on a camp or mission trip, but in your church.

Let's make today's journey a little different. Spend the rest of your time on your knees. Ask God to let His power and majesty be present in your church so people will be filled with awe and so God's name will be glorified and honored. Ask God to reveal Himself in an awesome way both in and through your church.

DAY 4
Acts 2:44-45

What genuine love and concern the early believers had for each other! They considered that all they possessed belonged to God and that He was free to use their possessions to meet others' needs. I guess they took Jesus' words seriously.

I've seen girls who share a room at youth camp or on a mission trip put all of their clothes in a big pile. They agree to give each other the freedom to wear whatever is in the pile. That was what the early church did. They considered everything they had to be common to all, but it wasn't just for a week (as it was for the girls I just mentioned). Isn't that amazing?

I wonder what would happen if the believers in your church and my church began to share all God has given to us. Maybe it's time for us to start the sharing.

Ask God to show you someone who has a need and how you can meet that need. It may cost you time, money, or one of your possessions; but remember, you've yielded your rights to God. Then go out and meet the need God lays on your heart. Pray about this today.

DAY 5

Acts 2:46–47

Amazing! The early Christians continued to meet together and share everything. It wasn't just a one-time thing. What's even more amazing was the result God gave them for living life as He told them to live. They enjoyed the favor of everyone. That doesn't mean life was easier or they didn't face persecution; but all people favored, trusted, and honored them for their faith. And these first Christians experienced joy as a by-product of their faith.

People were coming to know Jesus and being added to the church daily. It wasn't a baptism every few weeks—baptisms were happening *every day*.

Ask God to return the joy of His presence to your church. Ask Him to do whatever He has to do to allow your church to be a powerful witness for Him in your community. Ask God to bring people into your life who will join you in this prayer for His church.

HIS TRANSFIGURATION

MEMORY VERSE:

"While he was still speaking, a bright cloud covered them, and a voice from the cloud said, 'This is my Son, whom I love; with him I am well pleased. Listen to him.'" (Matthew 17:5)

INTRODUCTION

God has created some amazing things: Niagara Falls, the Rocky Mountains, Old Faithful, the Dead Sea, the Himalayas, the Gobi Desert, the Mississippi River, Victoria Falls, glaciers, oceans, beaches, lightning storms, sunrises, and sunsets.

God has also given people incredible creativity. People have used their God-given gifts to create some amazing things: Mount Rushmore, the Leaning Tower of Pisa, the Eiffel Tower, the Great Pyramids, the Golden Gate Bridge, Wrigley Field, and Disney World. (Okay, I know the last two are a little weak, but I enjoy them anyway.) How many of these sites have you seen?

Now, how many amazing things have you seen God do? Have you ever had the joy of leading someone to Jesus or watching someone ask Jesus into their lives? Have you ever seen God stop the rain? Have you ever seen God heal someone physically and in an amazing way? Have you ever seen God heal someone spiritually? What else have you seen God do?

This week our journey with Jesus will take us to a point in time when God allowed three of Jesus' disciples to see an amazing thing—the glory of Jesus.

Get ready to be amazed!

DAY 1

Matthew 17:1

One of the things I love about the Bible is its precision. The writers knew what they were talking about. God wants you to realize that His Word is more than just someone's made-up stories. It contains historical events. The places the Bible speaks of are real places: the mountains and valleys, the cities, towns, and regions—Bethlehem, Jerusalem, Galilee, and so on. All of these locations can still be found today.

It's great that we're able to trust the Bible historically. No other ancient book compares to the historical and archaeological trustworthiness of the Bible.

As you begin this new week with Jesus, how does it make you feel to know that the Bible is true, living, and trustworthy?

Ask God to teach you something new that will help you trust His Word even more.

DAY 2

Matthew 17:2-3

Imagine what Peter, James, and John saw. The word transfigured means "changed." Jesus changed right before their eyes, and they were allowed to see a small, physical glimpse of the real Jesus. In other words, they saw His glory. *Glory* is from the Greek word *dokeo*, which means "to reflect." What they saw was a reflection of God through Jesus. He was as bright as the sun!

Then they witnessed a conversation between Moses, Elijah, and Jesus. (I wonder what they overheard? Luke 9:30-31 says part of the conversation was about the coming death of Jesus.) It makes me wonder what He'll look like when we see Him face to face.

What will be your reaction when you finally see Jesus face to face?

What will be His reaction when He sees you?

If possible, look outside right now at some of God's creation. Tell God how awesome He must be if this bit of nature is only a small reflection of God.

DAY 3

Luke 9:30–31

There goes Peter again. He was so much like us. He wanted to build three shelters to prolong this glorious time. Peter attempted to postpone—or avoid altogether—the coming suffering that Jesus spoke about during His transfiguration. By staying on the mountain—a "spiritual high"—suffering could be avoided.

Have you ever wanted to stay on the spiritual high of a youth camp or a retreat and avoid going back to your day-to-day life? The spiritual highs God gives us are meant to strengthen us when we eventually return to the real world. Walking with Jesus daily is how your life develops a strong foundation that remains secure even during the tough times.

How do you usually attempt to avoid the difficult times in your life? What was the last spiritual high you experienced?

Ask God to use your spiritual highs to strengthen you to walk your day-by-day life.

HIS TRANSFIGURATION

DAY 4

Matthew 17:5-6

How would you react if you heard the audible voice of God? The disciples heard it, and they immediately fell facedown to the ground—in total fear. What a change from, "Hey, let's build three shelters and just stay awhile and enjoy your glory, Jesus," to "I'm gonna fall down right here, bury my face in the ground, and quake in fear."

What was amazing was the disciples' reaction to God's three simple statements: Jesus is My beloved Son, I am pleased with Jesus, and you should listen to Jesus. Imagine their response if God had been angry! They probably would have dropped dead. How powerful our God is! Aren't you glad Jesus bridged the gap between God and man? God's clear command to us is to listen to Jesus and obey Him.

Now that you're becoming more aware of who Jesus is, why should you listen to Him (read His Word) and learn to obey Him?

DAY 5
Matthew 17:7-9

The disciples heard the voice of God and fell on their faces. Jesus touched them gently and told them to get up and not be afraid. That's His desire for you, too. God allows intimate times with Him. Then He'll say, "It's time to get up and go into a world that needs Me. Don't be afraid. I will never abandon you."

Now what were Jesus' final instructions to the three disciples (and us)? Not to say a word about Jesus until He'd been raised from the dead. Guess what? He's been raised from the dead.

As a Christian, what are you most afraid of?

Based on what we've studied this week, how does God help you through this fear?

Recount to God what He's taught you this week. Talk to Him about it.

HE PREDICTED HIS DEATH

MEMORY VERSE:

"He is the atoning sacrifice for our sins, and not only for ours but also for the sins of the whole world." (1 John 2:2)

INTRODUCTION

Quotations have always profoundly affected people. Several years ago one newspaper columnist asked readers for their thoughts on the top 20 movie quotations that define our times. Here are some of them from the survey:

"I'll be back." (The Terminator)
"Show me the money!" (Jerry McGuire)
"Life is like a box of chocolates." (Forrest Gump)
"You can't handle the truth!" (A Few Good Men)
"Hasta la vista, baby!" (Terminator 2)
"May the force be with you." (Star Wars)
"There's no place like home." (The Wizard of Oz)
"Yeah, baby!" (Austin Powers)
"Bond...James Bond." (The James Bond films)

Of course, I would include "Are you gonna eat those tots?" (Napoleon Dynamite), but I wasn't asked. The point is quotations are important.

This week we'll look at one of the most important questions of all time: Why did Jesus come to earth? Why is this question so important? Jesus claimed to be the only way to know God, the only way to live life with meaning, and the only way to know what truth is (John 14:6). That has eternal significance for all people—especially you and me. Jesus was very clear about why He came to earth: "Just as the Son of Man did not come to be served, but to serve, and to give his life as a ransom for many" (Matthew 20:28).

Now there's a quotation that carries some serious importance!

For three years the disciples had followed Jesus. And they'd left everything to follow Him. They believed Jesus was the Messiah who would set up His kingdom on earth. They hadn't yet grasped why Jesus had come. Not to rule—not yet! Jesus had come to die.

In this verse, they caught the part that He'd die, but they seemed to ignore the part that He'd be raised back to life. Isn't that like us? We hear only what we choose to hear.

The disciples "were filled with grief." In their minds, all they'd given their lives for was coming to an end. They had no idea that by Jesus' death, the world would have the opportunity to find forgiveness.

What has it cost you to follow Jesus?

Have you ever felt as though Jesus didn't deliver what you thought He would?

At this moment God may have bigger plans than you can understand.

DAY 2

Matthew 17:22-23

Again, Jesus clearly stated that He would die and be raised from the dead on the third day. This time Jesus gave His disciples the details—He'd be mocked, whipped, and then crucified. Jesus was allowing Himself to be killed as the sacrifice for the sins of humanity.

Isn't it odd that the disciples didn't ask any questions? Jesus told them He'd experience torture, death, and resurrection on the third day, but the Bible doesn't record even one question from the disciples. Perhaps they didn't want to hear the brutal truth.

What truths from God's Word have you read or heard recently that you've chosen to ignore? Why?

Ask God to give you a discerning heart to hear and understand what He desires to teach you today.

DAY 3

Luke 9:43–45

Everyone was amazed by Jesus' actions. His miracles and His teaching thrilled all who were present. But Jesus pulled His disciples aside and reminded them again that He didn't come to do miracles—He came to die. And again the disciples were shocked and confused.

Read verse 45 again. The disciples failed to understand Jesus; they were afraid to ask Him about what He'd just said. Why would they be afraid to ask? They'd been with Him for three years. They'd asked Him about everything else—from how to pray to who was the greatest disciple among them. (We'll get to these moments in Jesus' life in Weeks 26 and 23, respectively.) Why was this situation any different?

Maybe they were afraid to ask because they were afraid of the answer. Jesus really is God. The disciples may have realized that God had a plan for Jesus and it might not be the plan they wanted for Him. They may have been afraid to let go and trust Jesus' plan for their lives.

What are some things you've wanted to ask God about but have been too afraid to ask?

Ask God what is on His heart. Be ready to trust in His answer.

DAY 4

1 John 2:1-2

John understood why Jesus had to come to earth: He was the sacrifice for the sins for humanity. Jesus came to die.

A Native American tribal chief was well known throughout his region for being upright and courageous. To help prevent thievery, he set up a punishment system of severe beatings for any theft crimes. A short time later, a thief was caught. To the chief's astonishment, it was his own mother. The tribe began to make bets as to what the chief would do. Would he have his own mother beaten? Or would he forgive her and allow her to escape judgment? To everyone's surprise, the chief had his mother tied to the post. The tribe trembled as they realized a severe beating would surely kill the old woman. But before the first crack of the whip, the chief stepped up, wrapped his arms around his mother's small frame, and took the beating himself. In the same way, Jesus came to earth to take our punishment.

How does it make you feel to know why Jesus came to earth?

Tell Jesus your thoughts about His death.

DAY 5

Matthew 20:25-28

Here you have it—words from the mouth of Jesus about why He came to earth. Although He's God, He didn't come to be served, but to serve others and to give His life (in other words, die) as a ransom for the sins of humanity.

But He didn't stop there. Read verses 26-28 again. Jesus desires the same for us. We are also called to serve others—not to be served. We'll find our real joy only when we do as Jesus did: Give our lives to serve and meet the needs of others. How can we do this? Only by allowing Jesus to meet our needs can we be free to meet the needs of others.

Let's see how brave you are. Take a few minutes and ask God to bring you to the point in your life where only He is allowed to meet your needs. Ask Him to give you opportunities to serve others who are in need.

THE PARABLE OF THE SOWER

MEMORY VERSE:

"Others, like seed sown on good soil, hear the word, accept it, and produce a crop—some thirty, some sixty, some a hundred times what was sown" (Mark 4:20)

INTRODUCTION

Wouldn't it be something if you could actually sit at the feet of Jesus and listen to Him teach? Imagine looking into the eyes of Jesus, hearing His voice, watching Him move His arms as He speaks, catching the words He emphasizes, and watching the way other people react to His teaching. That would be incredible!

We can't be transported back in time, but our journey into the life of Jesus this week will allow us to see some of His words. He was teaching by the Sea of Galilee. The crowd was so large that He had to get into a boat, row out onto the lake, and then teach those gathered on the shore. In this instance, Jesus taught the people using parables. Parables are stories that came from the lives of the people—stories about things like farming and fishing. But Jesus gave these stories unique spiritual truths.

I've always been amazed to see how a group of students can experience the same youth event but respond in very different ways. Some fall more in love with Jesus and their lives show a change. Some hear the same words but reject Jesus and remain unchanged. Others respond at first but then fall away after the event ends. Still others listen and politely ignore what they hear and see.

How do you respond? This part of our journey reveals that it's the condition of our hearts that determines our responses. Are you ready for a spiritual X-ray?

DAY 1
Mark 4:1-9

Road signs are crafted in different colors—yellow, orange, red, green—to catch your attention. Why? Because they share important information that can impact your safety. When your teacher says that what she's about to share is important, you'd better listen; you'll probably see it on a future test. When your parents call you by your first, middle, and last names, they want your attention. People use a variety of methods to let us know that what they're about to say is important.

The Bible is the same way. The words in today's passage, "Jesus began to teach...," are clues to be alert.

What condition would you use to describe your heart when it comes to receiving God's teaching? Healthy, pretty much okay, needs work, or heart transplant needed—stat! Write why you chose your response.

Ask God to prepare your heart to receive the information He wants to give you about the condition of your heart.

THE PARABLE OF THE SOWER

DAY 2

Mark 4:3–4, 13–15

Jesus discussed four different heart conditions as they relate to receiving God's instructions for life. Here the "seed" represents the Word of God. And the "soil" is how receptive your heart is to receiving and acting on God's Word. This week we'll look at all four kinds of soil (or heart conditions).

Today's Scripture deals with a sad heart condition: The soil on the path. People walk on the path, so many feet have hardened this soil. The path has no loose soil in which a seed can take root.

A possible parallel is a life that's been beaten down for many years by rejecting God's truth, thus making it difficult for God's Word to get through and take root. This person can still hear the seed (or Word of God), but it just lies there on the surface. Eventually the birds (Satan) come and eat the seed, and the person forgets the importance of the Word.

If this is your heart condition, then ask God to break loose the soil of your heart so you'll hear and act upon His Word.

Do you know someone whose heart is like the soil on the path? Pray for God to do the same to her heart.

DAY 3
Mark 4:5-6, 16-17

The second type of soil is rocky soil. Many students have hearts like this. They attend a youth camp, retreat, or worship service where they hear the Word of God. At the time they respond to God's call, but in the days or weeks that follow, they don't make the choices required to put down "roots" to their decision. Their decisions were based on emotions, not on a desire to make Jesus Lord of their lives. Many students don't even obey God's command to be baptized as a profession of their commitment. So when trials or temptations come, they have no foundation (spiritual roots); and the winds of life soon blow them away.

Are your roots deep or is your heart's spiritual condition rocky?

What are you committed to do on a daily basis in order to develop deep roots in your relationship with Jesus?

What are you doing to develop your relationship with Him so that when tough times come, you won't "check out" spiritually and let the winds of life blow you away?

THE PARABLE OF THE SOWER

DAY 4

Mark 4:7, 18-19

When I was a young believer at a college retreat, I told God I didn't care what it cost me, but I wanted to follow Him with all my heart and accomplish His mission for my life.

How about you? Will you become like the thorny ground? Will you allow a relationship or a desire for money and things to choke out your relationship with God and prevent Him from shaping you into who He created you to be?

Or will you hear the Word, respond, and begin to grow solid roots? What's in your life right now that's choking out your relationship with God?

DAY 5

Mark 4:8, 20, 23

Read verse 23 again. It's telling you—in very strong words—to listen. It really means: If you aren't completely ignorant, then listen to what I'm saying and act on it. It's just like your mother or father is calling you by your first, middle, and last names.

Look at the wonderful promise in verse 20. Allow yourself to hear the Word—put yourself in places to hear, read, and understand God's Word. But don't be a hearer only; act on what you hear. Then your life will bear fruit. Through your life, God will bring others to know Him, and you'll find great joy. In fact, that's the only way to experience genuine joy in life. Don't miss the magnificent journey of a life sold out to Jesus.

Which soil best represents your life now?

What type of soil do you want for your life? Since good soil doesn't just happen, what can you commit to do in order to develop—or continue to have—a heart of good soil?

THE DISCIPLES' QUESTIONS ABOUT GREATNESS

MEMORY VERSE:

"Sitting down, Jesus called the Twelve and said, 'Anyone who wants to be first must be the very last, and the servant of all.'" (Mark 9:35)

INTRODUCTION

"I am the greatest!" Muhammad Ali, former world-champion boxer was known worldwide for his exclamations of being the greatest boxer of all time. (Many agreed with him.) But who would you say are some of the greatest people who ever lived (not including Jesus)? Would you choose Abraham Lincoln, Alexander the Great, George Washington, Thomas Edison, Johannes Gutenberg, Mozart, Mother Teresa, Leonardo da Vinci, Julius Caesar, Billy Graham, Martin Luther, Babe Ruth, Florence Nightingale, Benjamin Franklin, the apostle Paul? Albert Einstein was voted the most important man in the 20th century. Would you agree?

This week our journey with Jesus takes us into the realm of greatness. Jesus Himself answered the question: "Who is the greatest?" He then proceeded to teach what true greatness is and how to live a "great" life. You may be surprised by what He said. Money, power, fame, good looks, strength, speed, and intelligence weren't included on Jesus' list of criteria for greatness.

In fact, to be great in the eyes of Jesus may mean you won't be seen as great in the eyes of the world. Since you'll be on planet Earth for maybe only 70 to 80 years—and you'll be with Jesus for all of eternity—in whose eyes would you rather be seen as great?

Put on your shoes, and let's take off with Jesus. He'll lead us and teach us about living a life that's truly great.

DAY 1

Matthew 18:1

Wasn't it just like the disciples to be worried about who was the greatest? According to Mark 9:34, the disciples argued about it. Do they remind you of anyone? We're always concerned with who's the best, who likes whom, who said what, and who left us off their party list. These are such silly things to worry about over the long haul of eternity.

But back to the original question: Who is the greatest in the kingdom of heaven? The kingdom of heaven is every area ruled by God—both now and in the future. The disciples asked Jesus this question for selfish reasons. They wanted bragging rights. They wanted to be able to say, "I am the greatest!" Perhaps they weren't so different from us.

Write down who you believe are the five greatest people ever (besides Jesus).

Why did you choose them?

What does it mean to be great?

Ask God to teach you what true greatness really is.

THE DISCIPLES' QUESTIONS ABOUT GREATNESS

DAY 2

Matthew 18:2-4

In today's Scripture passage, Jesus defined true greatness for us. And guess what? His definition was not the same as our culture's. Jesus said whoever humbled himself like a little child would become great. What a radical thought!

The beginning of true greatness is humility. In other words, you realize who you are compared to who God is. You're fragile; He's almighty. This causes you to become like a little child—trusting and free with your affection toward God. The result of this childlike state is a freedom to live your life to the fullest—as God created you to live. And it's this fulfillment that allows you to experience true greatness—which we'll unveil tomorrow. Don't miss it!

What's the toughest part about "becoming like a little child"?

Write down a few of God's characteristics.

Write down a few of your characteristics.

DAY 3
Mark 9:33–37

Jesus challenged His followers to serve others. In fact, Jesus took the challenge to a new level by telling them to be the servants of all. That's one tough command. But it's the only way to achieve real greatness. God has given you gifts and abilities so you can use them to meet the needs of other people. God designed you to find real, long-lasting joy through a relationship with Jesus—but that relationship is lived out by serving others.

What are some things you really enjoy doing?

How could God use your passions to meet others' needs?

Name two people who have a need you can meet. Spend some time in prayer for them and write specific plans to meet those needs.

Now do what you were called to do—go meet those needs.

THE DISCIPLES' QUESTIONS ABOUT GREATNESS

DAY 4

Ecclesiastes 3:11

We're wired for eternal purposes. Nothing else will satisfy us. God designed us to want our lives to matter; we're created with a desire to serve others and to help them find their eternal purpose in Jesus.

As you've studied the words of Jesus in the Scriptures, God has placed a burning in your heart. He's calling out to you, asking you not to settle for mediocrity. Step out in your relationship with Him; trust Him and begin the adventure of serving others. Don't buy the lie that it's all about you; trust God that it's all about serving.

What would stop you from following God's call to serve others? What gifts do you have that God could use to serve others?

Take some time to ask God to break your heart for the lives of others, to help you see them as He does, and to create some opportunities for you to serve.

DAY 5

Matthew 18:5-7

These are some tough verses. We aren't supposed to use our gifts in the wrong way—to cause others to sin or to lead them away from knowing Jesus. If we do, the consequences will be very serious.

The words Jesus used here were, "Woe to the [person]." The word woe means "overwhelming sorrow" and "heavy disaster." It's obviously something you want to avoid. Jesus, as God Himself, has seen some pretty awful things. So when Jesus says "woe," our response should be, "Whoa!"

A servant is described in Mark 9:33-37 as one who puts others' needs above her own, welcomes others who are weaker than she is, and seeks to meet the needs of others.

What are some steps you may need to take in obedience to what God has taught you this week about living a servant lifestyle?

Talk to God right now about those steps.

THE PARABLE OF THE UNMERCIFUL SERVANT

MEMORY VERSE:

"Bear with each other and forgive one another if any of you has a grievance against someone. Forgive as the Lord forgave you." (Colossians 3:13)

INTRODUCTION

Before we begin this new week on our journey with Jesus, let me be honest with you. The truth that Jesus will teach you this week is not optional. If you desire to walk daily with Him, then you must learn to forgive others—even if they've badly hurt you. I'm not saying you should allow them to continue to hurt you, but you must forgive them.

I recently began a discussion with my youth group by holding up a $20 bill and asking who would like to have it. As you can imagine, every hand went up. I told them I'd give it to someone, but first I had to do something to it. I wadded up the bill, and then I asked who still wanted it. Nearly all of the students put their hands back in the air. I took the crumpled $20 bill, tossed it on the floor, stepped on it, and ground it into the floor with my shoe. I asked again if anyone still wanted it. Once more, the hands went up. So I told them they'd learned a valuable lesson: No matter what I did to the money, they all still desired it because it didn't decrease in value. It was still worth $20.

That's how people are. Many times people are dropped, crushed, broken, and ground into the dirt because of their poor choices. But no matter what happens, a person never loses his value to God. In God's eyes each person is still priceless.

Yes, I did give the $20 bill to one "blessed" student that night. Enjoy this week's journey,

DAY 1

Matthew 18:21-22

Jesus had been teaching the disciples about serving each other and about responding to believers who fall into sin. Peter popped up and asked, "How many times do I have to forgive those who wrong me?" Then he tried to impress Jesus by saying, "Is it seven times?" Jesus came right back with, "Seventy-seven times." In other words, we're to always show forgiveness to those who wrong us.

Excuses don't impress Jesus. If you're going to follow Jesus, then He doesn't offer any other options: You're to forgive those who sin against you. This is a tough statement, but remember: God has called you to represent Him to others. And forgiving them is a big part of that. Represent Him well.

Is there someone you're having a hard time forgiving?

Ask God to speak clearly to you from His Word about this subject of forgiveness.

DAY 2
Matthew 18:23-25

"The kingdom of heaven is like..." What a way to begin a parable! Jesus said this is how the kingdom of God (the rule and reign of God) will look in your life. Then He told a parable to show what forgiveness and the lack of forgiveness look like—as well as the consequences of both.

Expect people to hurt you—don't be surprised when it happens. The important thing is not that others hurt you; the important thing is how you respond when you're hurt. In Jesus' story, the servant owed the king a huge debt of 10,000 bags of gold—which would have taken a lifetime to pay back at the average person's salary. However, the law demanded that either the king be paid or the debtor and his family be sold into slavery.

The king responded with forgiveness. How would you respond?

Have you ever been wronged or deeply hurt by someone? What was your response?

Was God honored by your response?

DAY 3
Matthew 18:26–34

After the servant asked for mercy in paying back his debt, the king had compassion on him and canceled the debt. Then the servant was faced with the same situation—someone owed him. But he showed no mercy and had the man thrown into prison. When the king discovered what the servant had done, he had the ungrateful servant cast into prison to be tortured until he could pay back all he owed.

So what's the moral of the story? You've also been forgiven a mighty debt—one that you owed to God. All your sins have been forgiven by Jesus' death on the cross. That's a huge debt you could never repay. Realizing you've received this great forgiveness, you're now free to also forgive others for their wrongs against you.

It's so freeing to realize you don't have to let other people take away your joy by holding a grudge against them. You can forgive because you've been forgiven.

Why is it so hard to forgive those who've hurt you?

How does knowing how much God has forgiven you help you to forgive others?

THE PARABLE OF THE UNMERCIFUL SERVANT

DAY 4

Matthew 5:23-24; 18:34-35

God's response to unforgiveness seems tough. But if you're a Christian, then all your sins have been forgiven. Christians who are unwilling to forgive others will pay a heavy price. They'll lose the freedom to experience the joy God desires for them just because they won't let the offense of another person go. How sad.

The question is not, *Am I able to forgive?* or *Does God want me to forgive?* God gives you no option but to forgive. Those words may be hard for you to hear, but the journey with Jesus is never easy. It's exciting and fulfilling—but not for the faint of heart.

Are you willing to commit to forgiving others?

Tell God about your commitment—or lack of commitment. If you need to forgive someone, then write a plan of action to show forgiveness to him right away.

DAY 5

1 Corinthians 10:31; Colossians 3:13

Whatever you do, you should do it in the name of Jesus. Honor His name in all your actions; after all, you bear His name: Christian. Colossians 3:13 is a powerful verse. "Whatever" means exactly what it says. It doesn't matter how bad the hurt is or what your grievance is—forgive.

How did Jesus forgive? He was mocked, beaten, and nailed to a cross, but He forgave people—even knowing that many would never accept His forgiveness. In the same way, you can't be responsible for others' responses. You're responsible only for your actions. You're called to follow Jesus. He leaves you no option but to forgive. Get out of jail free—forgive!

What has God told you to do about forgiveness based upon the truth He's shown you this week?

THE PARABLE OF THE GOOD SAMARITAN

MEMORY VERSE:

"He answered: 'Love the Lord your God with all your heart and with all your soul and with all your strength and with all your mind'; and, 'Love your neighbor as yourself.'" (Luke 10:27)

INTRODUCTION

I believe it's safe to say that human beings are wired to follow Jesus. That's the way we were created—we have a natural need for a relationship with our Creator.

I read a story in the March 26, 2001 issue of Newsweek that reported the findings of a research project reported in The Annals of Behavioral Medicine. This may surprise you, but the researchers discovered that churchgoers actually live longer and take better care of themselves than do those who don't go to church.

The research was conducted at the Human Population Laboratory in Berkeley, California. The researchers enlisted 2,500 participants for a long-term study starting in 1965 and ending in 1995—30 years later. The study found that those who attended church exercised more often, got more medical checkups, had more friends, and felt less depressed. Ultimately, they lived longer than those who didn't attend church.

It's funny—the Bible tells us that if we want to live long, fruitful lives, then we should be obedient to God. Now reliable research also supports the words of Jesus.

This week we're going to look at Jesus' answer to the question, "What must I do to inherit eternal life?" (Luke 10:25). Jesus gave the man who asked the question two answers: Love God and love people. Sounds simple, huh?

Let's get back on our journey and allow Jesus to teach us more about how to live life to the fullest.

DAY 1
Luke 10:25–28

I love reading the words of Jesus. An expert in biblical law came to Jesus and asked Him how to inherit eternal life. In other words, he wanted to know how to go to heaven. Jesus said, "You know the law. You're the expert. What does it say?" The man responded with what Jesus Himself said was most important (Mark 12:28-31): Love God above everything else in your life and love your neighbor as yourself. Jesus agreed and said, "If you do this, then you will have a life worth living here on earth and will live eternally."

To truly live the Christian life, you must make knowing God the priority of your life. The result will be loving people as God loves them.

Is your relationship with God the priority of your life? How can others tell?

What do you do daily to express your love to God?

DAY 2

Luke 10:27-29

Jesus told us plainly how to live. He told the expert in the law to follow the two greatest commandments—love God and love others. Like so many of us, this man tried to rationalize the "love your neighbor" commandment. He had no problem loving God because he recognized all that God had done for him. But to love others— especially those who are different, who are enemies, who smell differently, who act differently—that's asking too much, isn't it?

So the expert tried to limit the people he had to love by asking Jesus, "And who is my neighbor? You can't expect me to love everyone." Yes, Jesus expects just that. You may not enjoy being around everyone, but you're called to show love to everyone if you want to love God and live the life you were made to live.

Who are the most difficult people for you to show love toward? Why?

Ask God to develop in you a genuine love for others. Ask Him to give you opportunities to express this love.

DAY 3

Luke 10:30

The road from Jerusalem to Jericho was a windy, mountainous road. Robbers would hide out along the road to rob travelers as they passed by. Unfortunately, the man in this parable encountered some robbers.

People have extreme value to God—even people beaten up along the road of life and left half-dead. In fact, God loves people more than anything else. We often get caught up in our selfishness and begin to believe that God loves us more than He loves anyone else. Others? We prefer not to think about them. We think of people as too young or too old, too rich or too poor, too popular or too lonely for us to help them. But each person has as much worth to God as you do; He loves them just as much as He loves you. God loves them, wants to know them, and chooses to love them through you. You and I— we're priceless. And so are they.

Who is the most unlovable, unloved person you can think of?

Pray that God will bring someone into that person's life to show God's love. (It just might be you!)

DAY 4

Luke 10:31-33

Remember the Samaritan woman from Week 12? Samaritans were the ultimate losers of their day—despised by all Jews. Yet twice now we've studied how God chose to use a Samaritan to accomplish His will.

I believe God is telling us that it's usually not the coolest, most gifted, best looking, or most athletic person whom He chooses to use. Instead, it's usually the one who is obedient and willing to step out, trust God, and do what He commands. In fact, the priest and the Levite were much more religious than the Samaritan—at least it looked that way on the outside. But the Samaritan just believed what God said and did it.

Are you known at your school, home, and workplace as a teenager who loves God and acts like it? Why or why not?

DAY 5
Luke 10:34–37

So what can we learn from Jesus, through the story about the Samaritan, about how to "love our neighbor"? How about these:

- His compassion showed through his actions.
- He met the man's immediate needs.
- He used his own resources—he sacrificed—to meet the man's needs.
- He sacrificed his time—a most precious commodity—to help the needy man.
- He didn't question how the man got into the situation; he just met the need.
- He got personally involved; he didn't just give money.
- He gave sacrificially—two silver coins (two days' wages).
- He was willing to be involved over the long haul if needed.

What does Jesus say to you and me? "Go and do likewise!"

God says His Word never returns void. Ask Him what He desires for you to do with what He's taught you.

LEARNING TO PRAY

MEMORY VERSE:

"'This, then, is how you should pray: "Our Father in heaven, hallowed be your name, your kingdom come, your will be done, on earth as it is in heaven. Give us today our daily bread. And forgive us our debts, as we also have forgiven our debtors. And lead us not into temptation, but deliver us from the evil one."' (Matthew 6:9-13)

INTRODUCTION

Seeing God can help us see life simply. My son, Ty, has helped me many times through his honest words. Here are a few choice sayings:

> *Responding to how God speaks to us through the Bible, other people, and our hearts: "God will be able to talk a lot better when we get to heaven."*

> *When introduced to my friend named Rich: "How come he's named Rich if he has no money?"*

> *About God: "He really is my friend. I just forget about Him sometimes."*

> *On being sent to time-out at school: "Sometimes I just can't get the wild out of my feet."*

> *When asked why he wanted to be baptized at age six: "I want to get some of that juice." (He obviously wasn't ready.)*

> *Ty's wish for heaven: "I just hope that there are no boogers in heaven because every day my nose fills up again, and I have to pull them out."*

> *On people who make fun of others: "Just pull out a booger and give it to them. They'll be quiet."*

Most fathers love it when their small child talks to them. I stop whatever I'm doing and listen to my children. It doesn't matter if they say some pretty goofy things. I'm interested in what they have to say.

Guess what? God is extremely interested in what you have to say, and He longs to hear your prayers. He also has some pretty challenging things to tell you. Are you ready to start talking and listening?

This week we'll look at what Jesus wants us to know about prayer. Prayer has been defined as "just talking with God." Sounds simple, doesn't it? But there is something awesome about talking with the God who created the universe.

DAY 1
Matthew 6:5-8

If you've ever wanted to know how to talk with God, then keep reading. Jesus began by telling us how not to pray. He reminded us to pray, but not so others would hear us and believe we're spiritual. He encouragesd us to be truthful and not just babble phony-sounding words to impress God. The bottom line? Just be yourself. God knows your needs, and He's just waiting for you to call out to Him.

What's the most difficult part of prayer for you?

Ask God to teach you about talking with Him this week.

DAY 2

Matthew 6:9-10

Prayer allows you to feel the heartbeat of God. This is why Jesus was so specific on the basic elements of prayer.

Jesus pointed out two of these in verses 9-10:

- *Know who God is and honor His name. Jesus said to hallow (or show reverence for) God's name because He is our Father.*
- *Surrender your will to Him because He is God. We yield our lives to accomplish His will on earth as it's already accomplished in heaven.*

To approach God, first you need to realize who He is. You have to approach Him with respect and honor. God is our Friend, but He's also Holy God. Approaching Him in prayer can completely change your life's direction in an instant. You won't yield to Him until you realize that He's the Lord of all. This is the condition for your prayers to be life changing.

Honestly, who is God to you?

Why should you yield your will to Him?

Talk to God right now about what He's shown you so far this week.

DAY 3
Matthew 6:11

Jesus encouraged us to ask for our bread for this day—not future days. At first glance this seems odd. But on closer inspection, it's amazing. Jesus told us that we're correct in asking God for bread (the necessities of life) for each day as we need it. This daily trusting creates a relationship of dependence on God. It's a reminder that God is our sustainer. In fact, God sustains all life. God even provides for those who don't acknowledge His presence.

Do you seek other relationships or areas of life to fulfill you? What are they?

What could be the danger of seeking fulfillment from sources other than God?

Our prayers should acknowledge His role as Lord. Why? Because it acknowledges God as the only real "Meeter of Needs." Seek God to meet your needs.

Talk to God about your trust in Him.

DAY 4

Matthew 5:23-24; 6:12-13

Today, Jesus wants to teach you two powerful truths. Are you ready?

First, you owe God a moral debt (your sin) that He's already forgiven. Therefore, you must also forgive those who owe you (those who have hurt you). It doesn't mean you allow people to continue to hurt you. You may have to remove yourself from an abusive situation, but you're still supposed to forgive them as you've been forgiven—completely. Come into God's presence with a clean heart—with no sin unconfessed and no one in your life unforgiven.

Second, you must ask God to help you make wise choices each day. Ask God to help you avoid exposing yourself to things that tempt you to displease Him.

Are you holding on to any sins in your life? Do you have a grudge against anyone? Are you exposing yourself to any area of temptation? Spend some time with God about these matters.

DAY 5
Matthew 6:9–13

Let's review the foundation for a rich time at the feet of God:

- *Acknowledge who God is.*
- *Yield to His will.*
- *Trust Him to fulfill your needs.*
- *Confess any known sins.*
- *Forgive others.*
- *Ask not to be exposed to temptations.*

God tells us in Hebrews 4:16 to come boldly into His presence (if we know Jesus) and He'll always be ready to meet with us. What are you waiting for?

Pray the model prayer in your own words and with your own needs. Acknowledge God as God of the universe and God of your heart; tell God you'll obey what He's teaching you; make God your priority; tell God where you've displeased Him; ask God for strength to forgive those who have wronged you; and ask God to help you choose not to expose yourself to temptation.

WEEK 27

THE PARABLES OF THE MUSTARD SEED AND YEAST

MEMORY VERSE:

"He told them another parable: 'The kingdom of heaven is like a mustard seed, which a man took and planted in his field. Though it is the smallest of all seeds, yet when it grows, it is the largest of garden plants and becomes a tree, so that the birds come and perch in its branches.'" (Matthew 13:31-32)

INTRODUCTION

Your relationship with God is like a marathon, a lifelong race to become who God created you to be. At times it can be hard to continue walking with Him. He never said it would be easy, but He did promise to give you the grace and mercy you need to live the life He created you to live. He desires to reign in your life.

As God's kingdom spreads throughout every area of your life, it eventually overflows into the lives of others. What results might happen?

- *For starters, you'll fall more in love with God.*
- *You'll begin to see things about God that you've never seen before.*
- *You'll stop doing all the talking and let God talk to you.*
- *Your worship of God will become deeper and more sincere.*
- *You'll know more clearly what's really important as you began to see life through God's eyes and value what He values.*
- *You'll bring peace and calm to those you come in contact with.*
- *You won't be quite so demanding of your friends, and you will honor your parents in a more genuine way.*
- *You'll begin to understand your purpose in life—to love God with all your heart, soul, mind, and strength.*
- *The people around you will be drawn to Jesus through your life.*

This week as we look at God's kingdom—His rule and reign in your life—may your journey cause you to completely yield to Him.

DAY 1

Matthew 13:31–32; Luke 13:18-19

Have you ever seen a mustard seed? It's incredibly small. At a recent student meeting, I placed one mustard seed on every chair before the students entered. Everyone came in and grabbed a seat. After a talk on Matthew 13, I asked the students to stand and check their seats for the mustard seed. Everyone was amazed that they sat on the seeds for nearly an hour and never noticed them.

A mustard seed is tiny; yet after it's planted, it can grow to a height of 10 feet or more. One of the largest of all garden plants, it provides rest for birds seeking sanctuary.

That's what happens when we allow the kingdom of God, which is His rule in our lives, to grow in us. God's rule within us will expand to provide rest to others.

What are you withholding from God? Why would you want to withhold this area? Talk to God about this.

If you aren't withholding anything, ask God to use your life to spread His kingdom to others.

DAY 2

Luke 13:20-21

Have you ever used yeast to help make bread dough rise? A very small amount is all you need to cause the dough to expand and make a well-rounded loaf of bread. As the yeast permeates the dough, it has a tremendous influence—a chemical reaction that causes the dough to rise and puff into a loaf ready for baking. It's incredible just how small an amount of yeast is needed.

Jesus said that's how the kingdom of God spreads. As we yield our lives to God's rule, His kingdom expands through us into the lives of others. It continues to spread and exert a powerful influence on all it comes in contact with. Our job is simply to yield control of our lives to Jesus. His job is to use our lives to reach others. We get to spread it around by our words and our actions.

Who has God recently placed on your heart that you'd love to see come to know Jesus?

Talk to God about that person right now. Ask God to open her heart to Him and to allow you the opportunities to represent Him to that individual.

DAY 3

Matthew 22:37-39

There aren't any shortcuts to maturing spiritually or having the kingdom of God grow in your life. It only happens by making God your highest priority.

God gives us some spiritual tools to use so His kingdom can mature in us. We'll look at eight of these in the next three days. These are nonnegotiables for growth.

The first three are—

- *Expose yourself to positive influences that challenge you spiritually. Also, be accountable to someone (see Proverbs 27:17).*
- *Learn to obey God immediately (see Luke 5:27-28).*
- *Learn to love God's Word. Read it daily in order to feed yourself spiritually (see Deuteronomy 32:46-47).*

Spend a few moments asking God to prepare your heart to receive the information He desires to give you about the condition of your heart.

DAY 4

Here are two more nonnegotiable tools for you to use as you make the choices necessary for God's rule (His kingdom) to mature and grow in your life:

- *Spend time with God. Get to know Him personally (see Luke 5:16).*
- *Learn to let go of what's dragging you down and keeping you from becoming all that God created you to be. It's called repentance and it involves turning away from what hinders you and turning toward God (see Hebrews 12:1-2).*

Out of the five tools you've looked at so far, which one is the easiest for you to use? Why?

Which one is the hardest for you to use? Why?

Spend some time talking to God about this.

DAY 5

Matthew 22:37–39

Let's take a brief look at the last three tools God has provided for us to use to spread His kingdom throughout our lives and into the lives of others.

- *Make sure all of your relationships are right. If there is anyone you've wronged or feel bitterness toward, then find that person and make it right (see Matthew 5:23-24).*
- *Develop a servant attitude by choosing to do good things for others. Look for the needs of others and serve them (see Philippians 2:1-7).*
- *Tell others about the good news of Jesus Christ (see Luke 5:27-29).*

Which of the eight tools do you need to spend some time praying about? Do it now. People are waiting to see Jesus in your life, and time is short.

THE RICH YOUNG RULER'S QUESTIONS

MEMORY VERSE:

"But seek first his kingdom and his righteousness, and all these things will be given to you as well." (Matthew 6:33)

INTRODUCTION

Many years ago, Arabian horses carried the kings and queens of Europe. Master horsemen were sent to Arabia to choose the most perfect physical specimens they could find. The horse's muscularity, pride, gait, eyes, and coat were all considered. These horses were then shipped back to Europe to undergo a rigorous training program before the selection process would determine which horses would carry European royalty. The master horseman would train the horses for three months in every aspect of obedience and style. Reactions to the whistle commands of the master were of utmost importance. Failure to stop or go on command could result in injury or death to the kings or queens the horses were chosen to bear.

After three months of training, the horses were locked in their stalls for three days and allowed no food and very little water. At the end of the three days, food and water were placed downwind of the stables. As the aroma of the food wafted through the stables, the horses were driven wild by the smells. Finally, the master would unlock the stables and the horses would run for the food. But as they were running to the food, the master would blow the whistle command to stop. The horses that obeyed the command were the ones chosen to bear the kings and queens of Europe.

God desires to prepare you to represent His name to your world. Tests will come your way (usually in the form of circumstances or people) to see if you've really learned that truth. As you learn to trust and obey Him, God will give you opportunities to represent Him. That's when life takes on new fulfillment.

DAY 1

Matthew 6:25-34

Jesus mentioned pagans (those who choose not to follow Jesus) in this passage. Many of them chase after the next fashion, the newest car, more money, more awards/victories, a fresh relationship, a better job, the next high, or the newest computer game in order to find fulfillment.

Jesus told us not to fall for that lie. He challenged us to seek Him (His kingdom and His rule in our lives) first, and He'll meet our real needs. Yes, life will certainly have problems, but Jesus said to follow Him and trust Him. After all, He's God. Don't forget this truth. In fact, verse 33 is a wonderful verse to memorize: "But seek first his kingdom and his righteousness, and all these things will be given to you as well."

What do you worry about the most?

How would seeking God first in your life help you to worry less?

DAY 2

Matthew 19:16

People were constantly asking Jesus questions—sometimes to trap Him, sometimes to rationalize their refusal to follow Him, and sometimes because they honestly wanted to follow Him.

Today's questioner wanted to know what he could do to earn eternal life. The words eternal life here probably meant a satisfying quality of life and not just heaven. It's a great question—not only for the first century, but also for today.

Think about the people you know. They're looking everywhere, trying anything, going anyplace, and asking everything in order to find meaning in life. Guess what? The answer is found in Jesus alone. Nothing else will ever last or satisfy.

What questions about life do you hear your friends asking?

If you could sit down with God face to face, what questions would you ask Him about life?

You can't actually sit down with Him, but you can certainly communicate with Him. Talk to God about the tough questions you have.

DAY 3
Matthew 19:17-22

I love how Jesus responds to people. Because He knows exactly what they're thinking, He responds to their real heart questions, not just the verbalized ones. The man asked what he had to do to earn eternal life ("What must I do..."). So Jesus said if he wanted real life, then he must obey the commandments. The man replied, "Which ones?" Isn't that odd? He asked Jesus to list the bare minimum for gaining life.

Jesus listed six of the Ten Commandments, and the man claimed he'd kept all of them. Then Jesus responded in an amazing way: "Let go of what you value, and value me as your priority. Follow me! This is life!"

There's the answer—only by letting go and following Jesus as your life's priority can real life be found. Nothing else will do. The rich young man knew he could "do good things," but he didn't want to follow Jesus because his wealth was his priority. How sad to miss what's most important in life for something you can't keep.

What's keeping you from making following Jesus the first priority of your life? Why?

Is it worth it?

DAY 4

Matthew 19:23-26

Yes, it's hard to follow Jesus—especially when few of the people around you are also following Him. Read verse 24 again. The disciples knew a camel could not go through the eye of a needle, so they asked, "Who then can be saved?" (They were getting a little worried by this point.)

Jesus said that for people it's impossible, but with God all things are possible. This is critical! He's reminding us that we can never earn salvation, earn His love, earn this exciting life, or even earn the right to follow Him. Only He—God—can enable us to live this impossible life. This is why it's so important to make your relationship with Jesus the priority of your life. All you are, all you were created to be, and all you were created to do is based on your relationship with Jesus. Follow Him!

List the five most important things in your life. How does your relationship with Jesus rank?

Ask for His help in making your relationship with Him your highest priority.

DAY 5

Matthew 19:27-30

Peter was always so honest with his questions. Here he asked Jesus, "What's in it for us since we've given up everything to follow you?" Jesus said, "You get everything *and* eternal life."

Stephen Curtis Chapman said it best in the song, "What Kind of Joy." He pointed out how much joy life offers—even in the hard parts—when you walk with Jesus. If you have the CD, then listen to the song.

Spend time telling God about the joy of following Him when things are good—and when they're tough.

THE RICH YOUNG RULER'S QUESTIONS

THE PARABLE OF THE WEDDING BANQUET

MEMORY VERSE:

"'So go to the street corners and invite to the banquet anyone you find.'"
(Matthew 22:9)

INTRODUCTION

Throughout the New Testament, Jesus described Himself as the bridegroom. He described His church—us—as His bride. Jesus desires to pursue His people, provide for them, and present them pure and holy as His bride—the ones He loves and is committed to.

In biblical Jewish custom, the groom took his best man with him and went to his bride's home. Then he took her to the temple for the marriage ceremony. Afterward, a wedding feast began that could last for days. It was one of the highlights of life in the Jewish community, and everyone wanted to be invited. Food, fun, games, dancing, and conversation were all part of this incredible celebration.

The Bible is filled with references, parables, and analogies of weddings and marriages. In fact, out of all the symbols used to illustrate God's relationship to humanity, the two used most frequently are marriage and the shepherd and his sheep. In this week's study, Jesus used a wedding to teach His followers about the kingdom.

DAY 1

Matthew 22:1-3

A wedding was the highlight of the Hebrew social calendar. A wedding prepared by a king for his son would definitely be the one event of the year everyone would want to be invited to. It would be odd for someone to refuse to attend such a party after receiving a personal invitation to it. Yet, that's what Jesus described.

It amazes me that people refuse God's invitation to be a part of His family. It's the most exciting life possible (and the only life that's truly fulfilling), yet many still refuse. It's also amazing to think a Christian would refuse the opportunity to help others accept eternal life. God, in His grace, chose us—along with His Word—to invite others to come to know Him through Jesus. What an honor!

Why do some people choose not to accept God's invitation?

What do you believe is your role in helping others understand God's invitation?

THE PARABLE OF THE WEDDING BANQUET

DAY 2

Matthew 22:4-7; 2 Peter 3:9

God is so patient with us. Since He wants people to come to Him, He's delayed His coming and prolonged our lives to allow people time to decide what they'll do with His great love.

In today's Scripture passages, the king sent his servants out a second time to invite people to the wedding banquet. They shared details about the party, yet some people just went about their daily lives and paid no attention to what the servants were saying. Others mistreated or even killed the servants.

People still have these responses today. As Christians around the world invite people to come to a relationship with God through Jesus Christ, many refuse or pay no attention; and some even kill or abuse the servants of God. Eventually, the response of the king will be God's response. There is no hope outside of salvation through Jesus.

How did you respond to God's invitation?

Spend a few minutes praying for God to soften the hearts of friends who have not yet chosen to follow Jesus.

DAY 3
Matthew 22:8-10

Salvation is not free; it cost Jesus His life. The only condition for us to receive salvation is accepting God's invitation to yield our lives to Him. All are invited to come to know Jesus—everyone. It doesn't matter how good or bad we are; we can come to Jesus, be forgiven, and have the life we were created to live.

As you go to school, work, or practice today, watch the people around you. Notice how different everyone is. They're all invited to know Jesus, and you get to pass out the invitations.

What intimidates you the most about talking to people about Jesus? Ask God to give you obvious opportunities to invite others to come to know Jesus.

Pray for the courage to do what God has called you to do.

DAY 4

This is a difficult passage, isn't it? Many will ignore or refuse the invitation. Others will actually desire to be at the party (in heaven), but will refuse to enter the way God has planned—through Jesus.

In many royal weddings, the host required his guests to wear a certain kind of wedding garment. It's similar to a party today in which the host requires people to wear formal attire or a coat and tie. In this parable one guest didn't wear the required wedding garment, and he was thrown out.

The wedding garment one must wear to accept God's invitation is Jesus Christ. Unless one puts on the "righteousness of Jesus Christ" (accepts His forgiveness as the only way to salvation), He cannot enter the party (the kingdom of heaven). Some call it intolerant; God calls it salvation through grace.

Is there any reason God would have allowed Jesus to die an excruciating death if there were another way for us to go to heaven?

DAY 5
Matthew 9:35–38

Today's Scripture passage is different. Read it again. As you do, think about—

- *Students and teachers you noticed at school yesterday*
- *Family members who don't know Jesus*
- *People you work with*
- *Neighbors*
- *Close friends who don't know Jesus*
- *People you've passed on the street*

It doesn't matter who they are. Jesus sees people as helpless—as sheep without a shepherd, having no ability to face life's illnesses, accidents, or death. Jesus wants you to ask the Father to send workers into the harvest field in the part of the world where you live—to tell people the good news of Jesus.

Ask God to show you the people around you who are ripe for a spiritual harvest.

THE PARABLE OF THE WEDDING BANQUET

THE PARABLE OF LOST THINGS

MEMORY VERSE:

"'For the Son of Man came to seek and to save the lost.'" (Luke 19:10)

INTRODUCTION

In the fall of 1871, the great preacher Dwight L. Moody preached in a large church in downtown Chicago. At the end of his sermon, he decided not to give an invitation for people to come to Christ. Instead, he invited the people to come back the following night when he planned to offer an invitation. At that very moment, a fire alarm went off and the great Chicago fire of 1871 swept through the city. The fire led to the deaths of 300 people and left 90,000 homeless.

Moody never returned to that church to give an invitation for people to receive Christ. And for the rest of his life, Moody was haunted by the fact that he was never able to give an invitation for those people to trust Christ for their salvation. He pledged to God that he'd never again fail to give someone that opportunity.

People are at the very heart of God. In fact, God values people so much He'll use every opportunity to draw them to Himself. Before people come to Christ, God places people and events in their lives to draw them to Him. Even after a person comes to Christ, God continues to pursue him.

When you struggle and fall away from following God, get back up and run to Him. He values you above all creation. Now let's take that journey to the very heart of God.

DAY 1

Luke 15:1-10

Ever wonder what God thinks of you? These two parables clearly show God's heart. In the first parable, one sheep out of 100 was lost. The shepherd went after it and didn't stop looking until he found it. In the second parable, a woman lost one coin out of 10. She also searched and didn't stop until she found it. Then she threw a party just to celebrate finding one lost coin.

God pursues sinners with the same intensity. He values us so highly that when we choose sin, a job, sports, or anything else over Him, He still pursues us. That's amazing! Why does He do that? Because God knows He's the only One who can ever satisfy us.

What are your thoughts when you realize how much God pursues you?

Talk to God about your reaction to Him actively pursuing you when you fall away from Him.

THE PARABLE OF LOST THINGS

DAY 2

Luke 15:11–16

The parable of the prodigal son may very well be the most moving of all the parables. It began with a younger son who was tired of living at home and wanted freedom to do whatever he desired. So the father gave the boy his inheritance and the freedom to leave. An inheritance was normally given at the death of the father and not before, so the son's request for the money was shocking and offensive. It was as if the son was saying, "You are dead to me."

God does that. He gives you the freedom to follow Him or not. But like the younger son, we soon discover that nothing really satisfies us for long—except God.

Is anything tempting you to quit living for God? What?

How do verses 14-16 affect your desire to leave God's care and direction?

DAY 3
Luke 15:17-24

My younger son once visited a local amusement park with a friend and his father. At one point my son got separated from them, and he soon realized he was lost. He couldn't do anything to find the people he came with. Finally, he found a policeman, admitted his need, and asked for help. After an announcement on the public address system, my son was reunited with his friend and his friend's father.

In today's passage, the prodigal son realized he'd lost everything. He longed for what he once had: a warm caring relationship and a home with his father. The younger son traveled far to return home, and he hoped he might be allowed to at least serve in his father's house.

When the father saw the boy, he was still a long way off. In other words, the father had been looking for his son's return. Then the father actually ran to his son, kissed him, and threw a party to celebrate his return. That's God's heart for you and for those who live apart from Him.

Do you need to return to the Father today? Talk to Him about it now.

Do you know anyone who is living apart from the direction and love of God? Pray that person would return home like the prodigal son.

DAY 4

Luke 15:25-32

Not everyone was happy about the younger son's return to his father. The older son knew his brother didn't deserve forgiveness. After all, he'd taken everything he could from their father, and he'd wasted it. And now that he'd lost everything, he wanted to return to the comfort of home. The older brother may have also been concerned that the younger son would now want part of the older brother's inheritance. It's easy to see why the older brother believed he had a legitimate gripe.

The passage shows the pure grace of God. Grace is getting something we don't deserve. To the father, all that mattered was that his son had returned. Our Father loves you—along with others who don't know Him. Do they deserve God's love? No, and neither do we. Have they done things for which they should be condemned? Yes, and so have we. Our willingness to forgive others should come from God and His willingness to forgive us.

Have you withheld encouragement, fellowship, or inclusion from anyone when they "came back" to Jesus?

Stop now and ask God to forgive you for having a judgmental attitude like the older brother in the parable. Ask Him to change your heart.

DAY 5
Luke 19:10

This is a powerful verse that summarizes Jesus' purpose in coming to earth—to seek and to save the lost. Why does God leave us here after we become Christians? If heaven is really so great, then why doesn't God take us there immediately after we become Christians? Because we're called to be available to be used by God to fulfill His purposes on earth.

Remember what you prayed yesterday? Write the name of the individual who came to mind—or think of someone who fits into that category. Make specific plans to take some action that will offer you an opportunity to share Jesus with that person.

THE PARABLE OF THE VINEYARD WORKERS

MEMORY VERSE:

"For God does not show favoritism." (Romans 2:11)

INTRODUCTION

"It's not fair!" I've heard that phrase a thousand times in my life. To be honest, I've used that phrase myself when others have received the things I wanted. I guess we all want life to be fair.

But life isn't fair. Some of us have wonderful parents and some have abusive parents. Some are born with great health and some aren't. Some have higher IQs, better athletic skills, or more refined artistic talents than others. Some are born into free countries and some are born in places where martial law and totalitarianism are typical. Life is not fair. God is not fair—in the sense that God doesn't give the same conditions to everyone.

But God is fair. God gives each person the gifts to accomplish the unique mission He's given to her. We're all given the opportunity, if we choose it, to have God use our lives to honor His name and to represent Him to our generation. In that way God is fair.

If you're waiting for life to be fair to you, then you may end up bitter and angry. Learn to find your fulfillment in your relationship with God and in the mission He gives you. Do your best to honor Him. Ask God to help you rejoice when others succeed. Learn to let go of jealousy when others receive things you feel they don't deserve.

This week our journey takes us to a hard-to-accept parable of Jesus. It addresses our need for everything to be fair. Get ready to be challenged.

Before we jump into this week's teaching about the parable of the vineyard workers, let's lay a foundation: God doesn't show favor. God doesn't prefer some people or races or cultures to others. God gives everyone an opportunity to follow Him.

Before I became a Christian, I went to church for good luck. It doesn't work that way. Christians give their lives to God. You were bought with a price, and you belong to Him. You aren't called to follow Him so you'll get good things; you follow Him to know Him better and to make Him known to others. In so doing, you find great joy in living with Christ. Yet, this exciting life isn't the reason to follow Jesus; it's the natural result of following Him.

Think about it: Why do you really follow Jesus? What do you expect to get out of it?

Talk to God today about helping you see life the way He wants you to see it.

DAY 2
John 21:20-22

Now, let's lay another brick in our foundation of understanding life's fairness. Jesus had just told Peter to "feed my sheep." In other words, Peter's mission was helping others know Jesus (the Shepherd), and teaching (feeding) them to walk with Him. Peter (who was known for opening his mouth too often and too soon) saw John walking by and said, "Lord, what about him?" Peter may have wanted to be sure John didn't get more than he did.

Jesus' words are meant for us as much as they're meant for Peter: "What's it to you? You follow me!" We all have a part—a mission—in God's plan. Some will have it tougher than others. We're to follow Jesus and not let what happens to others determine how we follow Him. God plans for each of us. One day we'll see how this tapestry all fits together. Until then, follow Jesus.

Has there been a time when what happened to someone else seemed so unfair that it affected your walk with Jesus? If so, what was the situation?

Ask God to help you see what He's planned for you and to help you not feel jealous of what others receive.

DAY 3

Matthew 20:1-7

Now that we have a little foundation, let's build on it by looking at one of Jesus' tougher teachings, found in the parable of the vineyard workers. The landowner (God) invited people to work in his vineyard. In return, he paid them a denarius (usually one full day's wage). At different times throughout the day, the vineyard owner found other people to work for him.

God is constantly inviting people to know Him and be a part of His plan. Aren't you glad God doesn't quit calling people after they turn 21? If He did, then we'd give up sharing Jesus with our older friends and relatives.

Thank God right now for the grace (undeserved favor) He's shown you and for the patience He has with you.

How do you feel about those who become Christians later in life?

DAY 4

Matthew 20:8–16

This part of the parable reminds us of the older brother in the parable of the prodigal son. The ones who'd worked longer were angry that those who worked for fewer hours received the same wage. Look closely at this parable. Here are some important principles:

- *God is free to do what He wants. You can trust Him to be God.*
- *The workers who came first had more time to serve the master.*
- *The workers who came later missed the joy of spending more time serving the master.*
- *Our rewards are the same: eternity with God.*
- *Rejoice when undeserving people experience God's blessing. Remember, our rewards are the same: we all get to know God and spend eternity with Him.*

What's the hardest thing for you when God seems to bless others more than He blesses you?

Talk to God about your feelings.

DAY 5
Mark 10:28-31

Peter felt a little self-pity about how much he'd given up for God, and he wanted Jesus to pat him on the back.

For some of us, following Jesus will cost a lot. He calls some to leave everything and go overseas; some will serve Jesus in their hometowns. Some will give money; some will receive gifts. Either way, our reward is the same: Eternal life, plus life on earth that's a hundred times more exciting than we'd have otherwise. Yes, it does cost a lot to follow Jesus; but it cost Jesus a lot to purchase our salvation—His very life.

Have you ever had a pity party over how much you've given up for God?

If God allowed you a choice, then how would you like to spend your life serving Him?

What's your passion? Offer that to God. Tell Him you're willing to do whatever He wants you to do.

THE PARABLE OF THE VINEYARD WORKERS

HE IS THE RESURRECTION AND THE LIFE

MEMORY VERSE:

"Jesus said to her, 'I am the resurrection and the life. The one who believes in me will live, even though they die.'" (John 11:25)

INTRODUCTION

Corrie ten Boom survived difficult years in a Nazi concentration camp during World War II. When she was a child, Corrie took to heart a deep truth that her father passed on to her, one that helped her during the dark years. When she and her father would ride the train together, he'd give her the ticket right before she boarded. That way, she wouldn't lose it. He'd give her the ticket at the exact time she needed it—and not before. How beautiful is that? God is the same way with us. He'll give us the strength we need at the moment we need it—and not before.

We'll face incredible grief in our lives. What are some of the greatest griefs? The death of a loved one, the loss of love, extreme illness or injury, rejection, failure...the list goes on. The cause of grief really doesn't matter. At the moment of your deepest pain, God will be there, and He'll be willing to give you grace and mercy to walk through the experience. When times of grief come, God will have your ticket ready. Be ready to take it.

DAY 1

Jesus' friend Lazarus was very ill. So Lazarus' sisters—Mary and Martha—sent for Jesus. But Jesus delayed His return to Bethany, and Lazarus died. Your reading today picks up after Lazarus had been dead for four days.

To Martha, Mary, and the others, the situation seemed hopeless. They'd given up any hope that Jesus could act. In fact when Jesus arrived, Mary wouldn't even go out to greet Him. Mary may have been angry with Jesus for not coming when Lazarus was still alive.

In our grief, we can easily direct our anger at God. This week you'll learn how to turn to Jesus during times of deep sorrow instead of turning away from Him.

When have you experienced the most grief in your life?

Where was God during this time? How did you know?

Ask God to reveal to you more of who He really is so you can honor Him even in the tough times.

DAY 2

At times we're tempted to twist what Jesus said to fit what we want—not what God wants. Even Satan took Scripture out of context to try to get Jesus to disobey God.

In this passage Martha misunderstood Jesus. She believed Jesus should have arrived earlier to heal her brother. After all, Jesus had healed many strangers, but Lazarus was one of Jesus' closest friends (John 11:3). Unfortunately, Martha's trust didn't go beyond her immediate needs. While Jesus wanted to reveal His power over life and death and include His friend Lazarus in this awesome moment, all Martha could see was that her brother could have been saved by Jesus' more timely arrival.

Our narrow viewpoint often keeps us from seeing God's perspective—with eternity in mind. Ask God to give you an eternal perspective, not a temporal one.

What things might God want to do through your life during times of grief?

DAY 3

John 11:25-37

Jesus made an incredible statement: "I am the resurrection and the life." Despite Lazarus' death, Jesus claimed power over life and death. Martha's jaw must have dropped when He made that statement.

Martha called Jesus "teacher." In Jewish culture, rabbis (teachers) didn't teach women; yet Jesus taught women quite often. Jesus shattered any cultural norms that prevented people from knowing God.

Read verses 32-37 again and notice the different responses to Jesus. Some continued to blame Jesus for Lazarus' death; some were lost in their grief; some doubted; and some still misunderstood who Jesus really was. This sounds a lot like the world today.

How do you usually respond when you face deep grief or sorrow?

Does knowing that Jesus has power over life and death affect the way you deal with grief and sorrow? How?

HE IS THE RESURRECTION AND THE LIFE

DAY 4

John 11:38-44

Death is the great equalizer. Unless Jesus returns before you die, you will one day face physical death. No one is immune from it.

When Jesus demanded that the stone to Lazarus' grave be moved, Mary was concerned that the smell wouldn't be very fragrant. She had no clue whom she was talking with—Jesus, the resurrection and the life. Jesus prayed—out loud for all to hear—that the purpose of what He was about to do was so people would believe. In other words, Lazarus' resurrection had a much greater purpose than just the consolation of his two sisters. This miracle would reflect (glorify) God so people could come into an eternal relationship with Him.

Ask God to drive home in your heart and mind what you've learned about Him from this passage—Jesus is the resurrection and the life.

DAY 5
John 11:45-46

I love watching people respond to God doing great things in the lives of others. The way people responded when Jesus raised Lazarus from the dead is so typical of the ways people respond to Jesus today. When God does amazing things, people respond based upon either their belief or their refusal to believe in Jesus.

After seeing (just not hearing about) Lazarus raised from the dead after four days, many placed their faith in Jesus. The amazing thing was that others who witnessed the miracle went to the Pharisees and complained. Even today there are some who don't want Jesus to be who He is and do what He does. Maybe they know that if Jesus really is God in the flesh, then it will affect how they live. How sad that they'd choose to miss out on how life is meant to be lived.

How could God be glorified through times of grief in your life?

Ask God to use your sorrowful times to honor and glorify Him.

HE IS THE RESURRECTION AND THE LIFE

MARY'S ANOINTING OF JESUS

MEMORY VERSE:

"The Lord detests the sacrifice of the wicked, but the prayer of the upright pleases him." (Proverbs 15:8)

INTRODUCTION

This week our journey leads us to confront another tough question: *What part does sacrifice play in my walk with Jesus?* To be honest with you, there will probably be times in your life when following Jesus will require sacrifice. It may involve sacrifice of your time, money, relationships, selection of entertainment, or other areas. But sacrifice is vital for your spiritual growth and for discovering God's purpose and plan for your life. This week, God wants you to take time to prepare yourself to trust Him so you'll have a right attitude when He calls you to make sacrifices.

Remember—

- *God has given us the most incredible gift: An intimate and personal relationship with Him through Jesus.*
- *God has given us the privilege of having deep and honest relationships with other Christians.*
- *God has called us to represent Him to this generation.*

This week, take a few minutes to prepare for what God will teach you about sacrifice. Ask God to open your heart to realize who He really is— the Almighty God of the universe. Then ask Him to give you a humble heart that's willing to say "yes" to whatever He has planned for you. Finally, ask God to give you a tender heart that sees the world around you the way God sees it—a world looking for purpose and meaning that can be found only in Jesus.

The adventure you were created for awaits you as you follow Jesus with your whole heart.

DAY 1

Proverbs 15:8

This is a verse worth memorizing this week. Read it again. More than sacrifice, God desires for you to place ultimate value on your relationship with Him. Your heartfelt prayers please Him. God isn't pleased by sacrifice without love.

Read 1 Corinthians 13:1-3. God values a real relationship with you. You don't need to make sacrifices to impress God. Just be willing to sacrifice when God leads you to do so. And you don't have to look for places to sacrifice; life will bring them to you. Simply make God the priority of your life and be willing to trust Him when the time for sacrifice comes.

Have you ever made a sacrifice to God in an attempt to receive something from Him? What was the result?

Why does God desire your heart more than your sacrifice?

DAY 2

John 12:1-3

One of the Bible's most well-known examples of sacrifice is found in this week's Scripture passage—Mary poured expensive perfume on Jesus. He had recently raised Mary's brother, Lazarus, from the dead, and the event was still fresh in Mary's mind. Her heart was full of gratitude for what Jesus had done and awe over the realization of His mighty power over death. The stage was set for her willingness to make a sacrifice.

What things make you grateful to God?

What have you witnessed God do—both in and around you?

Thank God for your answers to these two questions.

DAY 3

John 12:3, 7

Mary's sacrifice was part of God's plan. She chose to make the sacrifice, but God gave her the opportunity to do as He intended.

Mary gave to Jesus what was possibly the most expensive item she owned. Pure nard was extremely expensive. This was not a simple $5 offering but a costly perfume she gave as a sacrifice. And she gave it without any possibility of repayment. It would be similar to you giving away your most treasured possession—whatever that might be—with no chance of being repaid.

Then Mary used her hair to wipe the perfume from Jesus' feet. The care of a guest's dirty feet was the responsibility of the lowest servant. Not only that, but the unbinding of a woman's hair in public might have been seen as less than respectable. So Mary not only sacrificed financially, but she also sacrificed her reputation to honor Jesus.

What about sacrifice scares you?

What more would you need to know about God in order to yield whatever He asked and whenever He asked for it?

Pray that God will reveal Himself and His ways to you.

DAY 4
John 12:4-6

Don't be surprised when you're criticized for trying to obey God. The hardest criticism comes from those who are supposed to be our friends. Judas Iscariot criticized Mary because the expensive perfume could have been used for the poor. (The truth is Judas was not interested in the poor; he saw an opportunity to grab money for himself.) If you spend your life serving God, then you'll probably hear someone say you're wasting your life. Most people value temporary things. Don't be discouraged by their criticism. God places great value on your service and obedience.

Can you remember times when people criticized you for following God?

Ask God to protect you from being critical and from listening too closely to the negative criticism of others.

DAY 5
John 12:7–8

God's call to sacrifice always has a purpose. You may recognize that purpose immediately—or you may not know what it is for years. But God always wraps your sacrifice in His purpose.

In today's passage Jesus linked Mary's sacrifice with His death, burial, and resurrection. Her one-time action had eternal results. You can never out-give God. (Read that last sentence again.) Mary made that discovery through the revival of her brother. Using the perfume on Jesus wasn't much of a sacrifice when compared to the life of the brother she loved dearly. Mary was ready to make her sacrifice.

Are you?

Ask God to check your attitude. Ask Him to prepare you for whatever He asks. Say, "Yes, God," before you know the question.

What area of your life is the most difficult for you to make sacrifices?

Pray for God's special work in your life so you'll value nothing more than Him.

HIS TRIUMPHAL ENTRY INTO JERUSALEM

MEMORY VERSE:

"God is spirit, and his worshipers must worship in the Spirit and in truth."
(John 4:24)

INTRODUCTION

What does the word "worship" mean to you? Everybody worships something. If a person doesn't worship God, then he may worship popularity, a car, his girlfriend, or his plans for the future. But everyone worships something.

As we continue to follow Jesus, His life and words take us to the topic of worship. Believe it or not, worship is not just what we do in church on Sundays. Worship is who you are and what you do. It's how you live 24/7. Worship is what you value—what your life and decisions revolve around.

And now a little word study for you scholars. Our word "worship" comes from the old English word *weorthscipe*. It's defined as placing the highest value on something. In the Old Testament, two Hebrew words are used for worship: *sahah* (to bow down) and *asay* (to serve). In the New Testament, three Greek words are used for worship: *latrough* (to serve), *sebomai* (to revere), and *proskuneo* (to bow down).

Therefore, worship can be defined as placing priority on one's relationship with God and valuing what He values. It involves serving, humbling oneself before Him, and showing reverence for Him by how one lives.

This week our journey will take us up close and personal with worship.

DAY 1

1 Corinthians 3:16; 6:19; 2 Corinthians 6:16

Did you get what Paul was trying to tell you in these passages? I know it sounds unbelievable, but when you ask Jesus into your life and become a Christian, God places His Spirit inside of you. That means your body is now the temple of God (the Holy Spirit). God doesn't live inside your church building; God lives in you. Worship isn't something you do; it's who you are. And since a temple is a location of worship, you should treat your body in a way that honors God.

What are your thoughts about having God's Spirit living inside of you—going everywhere you go and doing whatever you do?

Ask God to allow you to live your life in order that others may know Him.

DAY 2

Luke 19:28-35

Did you grasp what you just read? Jesus let His disciples know that He was in control of all situations. Even the colt Jesus would ride into Jerusalem had been prearranged.

This shows us that God is worthy of our worship and trust. He's in control. No matter how tough life may become, God's plans won't be thwarted. Even when circumstances are difficult, God is still God, and He's still in control. That means we can continue to worship Him in the good and the bad times. You can always trust God because He's always in control.

What area of your life is the most difficult to trust God with? Why?

Tell God about your struggles and doubts. Ask Him to give you opportunities to strengthen your faith in Him.

DAY 3

Luke 19:36–38

Did you notice that small phrase at the end of verse 37: "for all the miracles they had seen"? The crowd was joyfully praising God, but not because He was God or because He deserved their praise. They were praising God because of all the miracles they'd seen. To them, God was like Santa Claus. As long as Jesus was doing miracles and pleasing them, the crowd praised God. When things got tough a few days later, the crowd yelled, "Crucify Him!"

How quickly our praises can turn to curses when God doesn't give us what we think we need. It's also odd how the Bible refers to the mob in verse 37 as a "crowd of disciples." These same disciples all scattered as soon as Jesus was arrested.

Answer this question honestly: Will you quit following Jesus when He doesn't do for you what you think He should—or will you trust Him during the good and the bad times?

What makes you think you'll continue to follow Him even when He doesn't give you what you believe you should have?

Pray today that you'll follow Him—no matter what.

DAY 4

Luke 19:39–40

Whenever Christians start to praise and worship God, some religious people (in this case, the Pharisees) will typically criticize the worship. If a person's heart is far from God, then that person will find fault with those who are trying to worship God wholeheartedly.

Is this you? Is your heart so cold that your only solace is to criticize those who are trying to worship God? Look closely and you'll always find something wrong in every Christian. We're real people with real faults; but instead of criticizing, we should encourage. Jesus said if no one on the entire earth praised Him, then the very stones would cry out His praise.

Take a few minutes to pray for the body of Christians you worship with on Sundays (your church) and during the week (the Christians at your school or work). Ask God to use you as an encourager—not a criticizer—in their lives.

DAY 5
Isaiah 29:13

This is a tough verse. It's a warning for those of us who've chosen to follow Jesus. We can use it to evaluate our own personal worship. Jesus used part of this verse in Matthew 15:8-9 to point out hypocrisy in the religious leaders of His day.

The verse warns of two things for those who worship God. Coming near to God with only words is insufficient. Check your heart's attitude. We worship God with our hearts, not our mouths. And our mouths should report what our hearts feel.

Does your worship consist of following earthly rules that don't come from your heart (such as standing, singing, kneeling, and putting money in the offering plate)?

Where is your heart when it comes to loving and worshiping God?

Ask God to do whatever He has to do in order to teach you how to worship Him with your whole life.

THE PHARISEES' AND SADDUCEES' QUESTIONS

MEMORY VERSE:

"Therefore, rid yourselves of all malice and all deceit, hypocrisy, envy, and slander of every kind." (1 Peter 2:1)

INTRODUCTION

Many times the course of history has been determined by small and unforeseen events.

In the early part of the last century, Mao Tse-tung led a march thousands of miles into northern China. Thousands of Chinese soldiers became sick and many died. After they retreated, Mao contacted a mission-oriented Christian college in the United States and requested a team of physicians and medical equipment to work with the wounded soldiers. Mao reportedly told the university they could also preach the gospel without any hindrances. They'd also be allowed to pass out Bibles and do missionary work among the troops. At that time several missionary societies ran the university. Deeply grieved, the university declined the request because they were desperately short-staffed—only one surgeon was at the school at the time. With that refusal a priceless, never-since-repeated opportunity to spread the gospel in that region was lost.

I wonder what would have happened if a team of believers had been ready to go to communist China when the doors opened. What would have happened if Mao Tse-tung had been converted to Christianity? This week ask yourself, *Am I ready to go when God opens the doors?*

DAY 1

1 Peter 1:22–2:3

God wants you to be ready—ready for Him to use you when He opens doors for you and asks you to represent Him to others. How do you start? Read today's passage again. Peter assumes you're born again and you strive to obey God's Word. He assumes you love your brothers and sisters in Christ. Peter calls you to rid yourself of hypocrisy. Hypocrisy is the "pretense of having characteristics one does not possess or the deceitful assumption of virtue." In other words, hypocrisy is verbally claiming to be one thing but not showing it with your actions. This week our journey with Jesus takes us face-to-face with the H word—hypocrisy.

Would it bother you if someone called you a hypocrite? Why?

Why is being a hypocritical Christian so damaging to the name of Jesus?

DAY 2
Matthew 22:34-40

What's more important on an airplane—the left wing or the right wing? It doesn't take Sherlock Holmes to guess the answer: Both are important. If either wing falls off, then the plane cannot fly.

What's more important for a Christian: The words she says or the life she lives? Is it words or actions? Obviously, both are essential. If you live the Christian life but never verbalize why (e.g., "because of Jesus"), then you'll be known only as a nice, moral person. If you talk about Jesus but never walk the walk, then you'll be known as a phony. The first life will probably lead very few to Jesus; the second life will lead no one to Him. Words and actions go hand in hand. Actions open the door, and words show the way.

Do you struggle more with your words or your actions? Why?

Ask God to develop in you a deep love for Him that's obvious to those around you.

DAY 3
Matthew 22:15-22

The Pharisees were religious leaders who knew all the "Bible answers" but didn't live the way the Bible said they should. They were hypocrites.

The Pharisees were also naturalists (against Roman rule), while the Herodians supported King Herod (a puppet king set up by Rome) and were in favor of Roman rule. But these two opposing groups joined together to trap Jesus because they both feared what He was teaching. In today's passage they asked Jesus a trick question they believed would cause Him to support Caesar and Roman rule (instead of Israel) or speak out against Rome. Either way, Jesus would lose.

They dropped the big question: "Do we pay taxes to Caesar (support Rome) or not (go against Roman rule)?" If Jesus answered "yes," then the Pharisees would denounce Him as being disloyal to His nation, Israel. But if He answered "no," then the Herodians would report Him to the Roman governor as a traitor.

Jesus grabbed a coin and asked whose face was on it. When they replied, "Caesar's," Jesus said, "So give back to Caesar what is Caesar's [the money], and to God what is God's."

Okay, so what does God want? He wants your life—your words, heart, and actions.

Does God have your words, heart, and actions? If not, why not?

DAY 4

Matthew 23:1-12

Wow! This is tough. Jesus spelled out what a hypocrite does, using the Pharisees as examples:

- *They sit in the temple (church) and love to be taught and to teach.*
- *They tell others what they should do, but they don't do it themselves.*
- *They put guilt trips on others, but they don't live the life they talk about.*
- *They do their religious stuff so others will see them.*
- *They dress up to look holy; they wear all the right clothes.*
- *They love being part of the religious in-group at church and at school.*
- *They don't humble themselves and serve others—especially the lonely, hurting, and outcast.*

It's not a pretty picture, especially to God.

Does this paint a picture of you?
Which part bothers you the most? Why?

Ask God to show you the areas in which you may have become hypocritical. Spend a few minutes before God on this issue.

DAY 5

Matthew 23:24–28, 37–38

God takes hypocrisy very seriously. He doesn't want your life to hinder others from coming to know Him. Instead, God wants people to want to know Him better because of your influence.

Jesus compared hypocrites to tombs. Go by a cemetery this week. You'll see beautiful gravestones. Yet inside those graves are dead bones. That's a hypocrite—pretty on the outside, rotten on the inside.

So would you guess that Jesus wanted to "zap" the hypocrites? No! Read verses 37-38 again. God wanted them to quit being hypocritical and to follow Him. Jesus always gives us the choice. What a wonderful Savior!

What are some specific areas of your life in which you're being a hypocrite?

Ask God to forgive and cleanse you as you turn away from that behavior. Ask for help and accountability not to be a hypocrite.

WEEK 36

SIGNS OF THE END TIMES

MEMORY VERSE:
"Therefore keep watch, because you do not know on what day your Lord will come."
(Matthew 24:42)

INTRODUCTION

From the start, the movement was doomed to fail. For one thing, "it began with just 120 men...most of the men were illiterate and poor...The strategy of the movement was disastrous. No headquarters was ever established. No professional research was ever done. Plans were made by the seat of the pants. The leaders couldn't even agree on the exact definition of their mission...The movement was doomed to failure. But it didn't fail."[1]

Read these verses from Psalm 66:5-9 and praise God for choosing you to be a part of His plan for the world:

> Come and see what God has done,
> his awesome deeds for mankind!
> He turned the sea into dry land,
> they passed through the waters on foot—
> come, let us rejoice in him.
> He rules forever by his power,
> his eyes watch the nations—
> let not the rebellious rise up against him.
>
> Praise our God, all peoples,
> let the sound of his praise be heard;
> he has preserved our lives
> and kept our feet from slipping.

What a great God we serve, and what a privilege to be a part of the greatest movement in the history of the world.

---

1 Max Lucado, *On the Anvil: Stories on Being Shaped into God's Image* (Carol Stream, Ill.: Tyndale House, 1985), 115-116.

DAY 1

Matthew 24:3

When the disciples got Jesus alone, they asked the question nearly all Christians have asked ever since: "When are you coming back?" It's a great question, for sure.

Wouldn't it be something if our generation was the one God chose to usher in Jesus' return? That would be fantastic for two reasons: We'd get to see it happen with our own eyes, and we wouldn't have to taste physical death. But whether it happens on our watch or not, Jesus tells us to be ready for it at all times.

What crosses your mind when you think about Jesus coming to earth again?

Are you ready for that to happen? Why or why not?

Talk to God about how you answered that last question.

DAY 2

Matthew 24:4-8

Jesus strongly encouraged His disciples not to be deceived by those claiming to be Christ or claiming to have special knowledge of His return. Many people, especially in the last 200 years, have claimed special knowledge of His second coming. Obviously, they've all been wrong.

Wars, earthquakes, and famine will occur—and will even occur more frequently—during the last days. Even so, Jesus warned us that this wouldn't be the end. An increase in worldwide tragedies is only the beginning of the end. Over the last several years, and despite all our modern technology and claims of tolerance, we've seen an increase in famines, floods, earthquakes, terrorism, and other tragedies. Don't be alarmed. Continue to walk with Jesus and spread the news of His offer of eternal life. Remember, we belong to God, and He has everything in His control.

Which world problems alarm you the most?

Thank God that He's in control and praise Him for His power.

DAY 3
Matthew 24:9-14

Today we'll look at a good news-bad news scenario for the end times. First, the bad news: Most Christians, maybe even you, will face persecution as they enter the last days. False prophets will attempt to discredit Jesus and deceive people. Many will turn away from the faith and ridicule those who continue to follow Jesus. Verse 12 in today's passage says evil will increase. A good example of this is how the creators of movies and TV shows continue to increase the levels of immorality in their programs, while making fun of those who ask for programs that don't flaunt immorality.

Now, the good news: In spite of all the bad news that exists today, the gospel will be preached to the whole world, and then the end will come. And many people will see the truth and come to Jesus. You and I are invited to be a part of God's plan.

What's the hardest part about staying alert for Jesus' return?

Thank God that He's sovereign (always in control).

DAY 4

Matthew 24:30–35

Don't be caught by surprise. When Jesus comes again, those who've rejected Him, delayed giving their lives to Him, or denied who He is will mourn. The word mourn actually means to wail and grieve.

As for the followers of Jesus, He'll send His angels to gather us from all over the earth. What an awesome experience that will be! The generation that's alive when that event comes to pass will be truly blessed.

Are there people you'd love to see come to know Jesus so they won't miss being a part of His return? Make a list of their names and continue to pray for their salvation.

Matthew 24:36-44

While there is much about Christ's return we cannot know, there are a few things we can:

- *No one (except God) knows what day Jesus will come to earth again—not even Jesus!*
- *Jesus will come quickly (in the "twinkling of an eye").*
- *His return will surprise most people.*
- *Because He'll come when we don't expect Him, Jesus wants us to stay alert, keep watch, and be ready. In fact, Jesus even said we "must be ready" (verse 44).*

Here's a final warning: Don't be deceived by those who claim to know when Jesus is coming back to earth. If someone tells you that, then you can be sure it's foolishness.

Our journey ends with a common greeting shared among the early believers: Maranatha! (The Lord is coming back soon!)

What about Jesus' return excites you most?

Are you ready? Why or why not?

Ask God to show you how to live in anticipation of Jesus' return.

HIS LAST SUPPER WITH HIS DISCIPLES

MEMORY VERSE:

"This is my blood of the covenant, which is poured out for many for the forgiveness of sins." (Matthew 26:28)

INTRODUCTION

Here are some unusual events described in the Bible:

- *Genesis 5:27—A man named Methuselah lived to be 969 years old.*
- *Numbers 22:28-30—A donkey spoke to a man.*
- *Joshua 10:13—The sun stood still for an entire day.*
- *Judges 4:17-21—A woman killed a man by driving a tent peg through his head.*
- *Judges 20:16—An army included 700 left-handed men.*
- *2 Kings 6:1-6—An iron axhead floated on the water.*
- *2 Chronicles 11:21—A father had 88 children.*
- *Isaiah 20:2-3—A man walked around naked for three years.*
- *Isaiah 38:8—The sun traveled backward.*
- *Matthew 1:1-5—A prostitute was an ancestor of Christ.*
- *Matthew 3:4—A man ate locusts.*

The Bible is full of unusual stuff, but here's another interesting thing we could add to the list: God became human and came to earth to die for humanity's sins. What's more unusual than that?

Why did Jesus have to die? Why couldn't God, in all His power, just say He'd forgive anyone who called upon His name? Why did there have to be a sacrifice—the death of God's Son? These are tough questions. Our journey to know Jesus better will cause us to take a hard look at the answers to these questions.

Enjoy your week with Jesus.

DAY 1

Matthew 20:28; Matthew 26:28; Acts 2:22-24

Why did Jesus have to die? He died as a payment for our sins. He wasn't murdered. No one trapped Jesus. Jesus didn't make a miscalculation. The cross didn't surprise Him. Nothing went wrong when He was crucified; in fact, everything went exactly right. The way Jesus walked to His death should leave no doubt in our minds that He came to earth for that very moment. We have forgiveness of our sins and eternal salvation as a result of His willingness to die on a cross for us.

In your own words, write how you feel about Jesus' death on the cross providing a way for all your sins to be forgiven and forgotten by God.

Even though the answer to "Why did Jesus have to die?" is clear, it should still cause us to look deeper into God's heart. Ask God to prepare you for the answers as we continue.

DAY 2

Jesus' death revealed two important characteristics of God: His love and His justice. You cannot separate the two. God's justice requires a payment for our sinful actions. Yet justice is an impartial application of the Law. God's Law states the wages of sin is death (Romans 6:23). That means the penalty for our sin is death. Either we pay that penalty, or someone has to pay it for us—but who would do that?

Jesus—God in the flesh—took that penalty of death in our place. He died instead of us. His awful, painful death clearly shows how much God hates sin—yet loves us. Why does God hate sin? Because He knows it will destroy us and all He created us to be. God's justice demands a payment for sin—and God's love sent Jesus to the cross to pay it.

In your own words, why did Jesus have to die? Why couldn't God just say, "I forgive you"?

Even though we cannot understand all the ways of God, we can certainly understand that He loves us enough to send His Son to die for us. Thank God for that gift.

DAY 3
John 3:16; 15:13; Romans 5:8

Jesus had to die to show us that God loves and values us. Today's verses clearly state Jesus' death was an expression of God's love for all humanity. God becoming a man and dying by horrible Roman crucifixion is the strongest act of love the world has ever known. This Almighty God of the universe became one of us, and then He died for us. What an awesome act of love!

If there were any other way for us to get to heaven, then God would not have made such a huge sacrifice. This great act of love is the only way to be forgiven for sin.

Who is one person you'd like to see come to know Jesus?

Ask God to help you. Then look for an opportunity to share with that person about the meaning of Jesus' death on the cross.

DAY 4

Matthew 26:26-30; 1 Corinthians 11:23-26

As a reminder of the most important event in all of history, Jesus gave a command to remember His death and sacrifice by observing the Lord's Supper (Communion). We break and eat the bread as a reminder of Jesus' body being broken for us. We drink the juice as a reminder of His precious blood being shed for us for the forgiveness of sins. Eating the bread and drinking the juice is a clear remembrance of His death, but also a reminder that we must make the choice to accept God's forgiveness and ask Jesus to come into our lives. It's a personal choice.

The next time your church observes Communion, ask God to bring to your mind the great sacrifice He made for your salvation. First Corinthians 11:25 refers to the shedding of Jesus' blood as a "new covenant." A covenant is a binding agreement between two or more parties. Jesus' blood is the symbol of God's promise to us.

What would make the observance of Communion more meaningful to you?

DAY 5
Matthew 16:24–26

So what do the truths we've learned this week mean to us? Jesus now calls us—and anyone who wishes to be His disciple—to take up our crosses and follow Him. A person on a cross has these characteristics:

- *He can look in only one direction.*
- *His own will doesn't matter anymore.*
- *He can do only one thing—bear his cross.*
- *His future plans are insignificant.*
- *He can never look back.*
- *He has only today; tomorrow doesn't matter.*

Jesus doesn't ask us to do anything He hasn't already done. Even when His requests seem demanding, our suffering cannot compare to what He went through.

Have you taken up your cross to follow Jesus? Why or why not?

Ask God to guide you to love and trust Him so that you yield everything to Him.

HE WASHED HIS DISCIPLES' FEET

MEMORY VERSE:

"I have set you an example that you should do as I have done for you."
(John 13:15)

INTRODUCTION

When Peter's mother-in-law became sick, Jesus healed her (Matthew 8:13-15). When the Pharisees attacked Jesus' disciples for "working" (eating grain in a field) on the Sabbath, Jesus defended the disciples (Matthew 12:1-3). When the disciples were terrified of a storm that blew up while they were crossing the sea, Jesus calmed the storm (Matthew 8:23-27).

Jesus was God in the flesh, yet He called the disciples His friends. When Jesus prepared to eat the Passover feast with His disciples, He wrapped a towel around His waist and washed their dirty feet in a great act of servanthood (John 13:1-11).

When showing us how to live, Jesus didn't just say, "Do the best you can." Rather, He lived His life in front of us so we could see how real life is supposed to be lived.

He asks us if we're ready to live real life—the kind that's so exciting, joyful, and full of purpose that others will want what we have. This life begins by making your personal relationship with Jesus your foremost priority. This life is lived out by serving others.

But here's the catch: You have to make the choice to live this kind of life—and it isn't easy. Read Deuteronomy 30:15-20 and make the choice.

Life gets exciting when we learn to love and serve others. In this week's journey we'll learn from Jesus about serving others.

DAY 1
Matthew 22:37–39; John 13:1-2

What is your purpose in life? Jesus said in verse 37 that our purpose is to "love the Lord your God with all your heart and with all your soul and with all your mind." You were created to love God as the top priority in your life. Nothing else will ever satisfy you for long. But how does this love play itself out in our daily lives? One way is how we love and serve others.

In John 13, Jesus showed His disciples the full extent of His love by serving them. Verse 2 is a stark reminder that the choice to love is ours. The devil didn't force Judas to betray Jesus; the choice was Judas' to make. The choice to follow Jesus is yours to make as well.

What's your first thought when you realize Jesus commands you to serve others?

Ask God to give your heart a desire to serve others.

DAY 2

John 13:3-5

Jesus provided the perfect example of how we're to serve. In fact, Jesus modeled whatever He called us to do. Serving others involves giving up our rights so we can meet their needs. It involves humbling ourselves and considering others to be just as important as we are. Jesus knew He was God, He knew all things were under His control, and He knew He'd go back to God. Even with all this power and knowledge, Jesus willingly put aside His rights as God and took the position of a servant in order to meet the needs of the disciples.

The lowest servant in a household was typically the one who washed the dirty feet of the master's guests. But Jesus—God in the flesh— took on that menial job. Jesus calls us to do the same. God created us to serve.

On a scale of 1 to 10 (with 1 being the worst and 10 being the best), how would you rate yourself as a servant?

What's the hardest part of serving?

What needs to happen in your life for you to please God by serving others?

DAY 3

John 13:6-11

Imagine Jesus—God in the flesh—asking to wash your dirty feet. Back in Jesus' day, most people's feet were dusty or muddy from walking on the dirt roads. So the first thing a guest would do when entering a house was remove his sandals. Then a household servant usually washed the guest's feet.

Jesus cleanses our lives and forgives our sins when we make the choice to become Christians. After we've made that choice, we need to yield ourselves to Jesus—give Him control of our lives—each day. We must allow Jesus to "wash our feet" (as well as our minds and hearts) daily.

Is there any hidden sin in your life that may prevent you from seeing the opportunities God gives you to serve others?

Spend some time with God and ask Him to reveal any sin in your life. As He does, turn away from that sin and repent of it. It's time to serve.

DAY 4

John 13:12–17

After Jesus washed the feet of the disciples, He commanded them to do the same for others. His command to us is the same. We should be willing to perform the most menial tasks in order to serve others.

How about you? When was the last time you served someone? Have you ever stayed after church or youth group to help pick up? Have you ever spent time with a student who isn't considered cool? Have you offered to serve your parents by washing the dishes, vacuuming the house, or mowing the yard? Have you given your time to serve others on a mission project? Isn't it about time you made the choice to serve? After all, Jesus is our example, isn't He?

Spend some time asking God to bring to your mind people and opportunities to serve. Write down whatever comes to mind. Then make the choice to follow through on what God shows you.

DAY 5

Mark 10:42-45

Plain and simple, Jesus came to serve. And He really does expect the same from you. It's so easy to serve God in the limelight when everyone is watching and patting you on the back saying, "Good job! Thanks for doing this." But how would you handle it if God called you to do some dirty, menial task day after day, week after week, and year after year in a place where nobody saw you doing it? Could you do it just because God called you to serve?

Are you ready to experience real joy? Then be ready to serve.

Commit to one action today, and after you've prayed that your action will honor God—do it! Then share the results with your small group leader, youth pastor, or youth group!

HE WASHED HIS DISCIPLES' FEET

THE GIFT OF
THE HOLY SPIRIT

MEMORY VERSE:
"But the Advocate, the Holy Spirit, whom the Father will send in my name, will teach you all things and will remind you of everything I have said to you." (John 14:26)

INTRODUCTION

God gives us life through Jesus. As God in the flesh, Jesus modeled how we should live. God gave us His Word for our handbook, but God didn't stop there. God also gave us the Holy Spirit to live inside us, walk with us, and give us the power to live.

Consider what God has given us in Jesus and through the Holy Spirit:
- *We're forgiven and made righteous (Romans 5:11).*
- *We died with Christ to the power of sin in our lives (Romans 6:1-7).*
- *We're free from condemnation (Romans 8:1).*
- *We've been given the mind of Christ (1 Corinthians 2:16).*
- *We've been bought with a price, and we belong to God (1 Corinthians 6:19-20).*
- *We've been blessed with every spiritual blessing (Ephesians 1:3).*
- *We've been made alive with Christ (Ephesians 2:4-5).*
- *We have direct access to God through the Holy Spirit (Ephesians 2:18).*
- *We have Christ living in us (Colossians 1:27).*
- *We've been made complete in Christ (Colossians 2:10).*
- *We've been given a spirit of power, love, and self-discipline (2 Timothy 1:7).*
- *We've been saved and set apart according to God's work (2 Timothy 1:8-9; Titus 3:5).*
- *We have the right to come boldly before the throne of God to find mercy and grace in time of need (Hebrews 4:16).*
- *We've been given exceedingly great and precious promises from God (2 Peter 1:3-4).*

INTRODUCTION *(cont.)*

And these are just a few of the things God has done in our lives! Our response should be to love God and yield our lives to Him.

This week's journey will lead us to look at the gift of the Holy Spirit.

DAY 1

John 14:12-14

What a tremendous Scripture passage! If we have faith in Jesus, then He'll do even greater things through us than He's already done. How? Jesus is with the Father, and God has sent the Holy Spirit to us. Through faith, prayer, and the power of the Holy Spirit, God allows us to do even more than Jesus did. Jesus said so Himself.

Don't miss the point here. God may do some amazing miracles that He allows you to witness. But even if He heals a person's cancer or provides thousands of dollars for an important ministry, that healed person will still die someday and that ministry will need more money down the road.

The most amazing things you'll see God do are eternal. They involve the eternal destinies of your friends and family being changed because they find faith in Christ. And God is willing to use you to make those miracles happen.

Ask God to reveal some of the desires He has for your life.

DAY 2

John 14:15

Before we look closer at the Holy Spirit, let's stop for a day and answer a difficult question: *How do you know if you really love Jesus?* It's a good question, and Jesus gave a clear answer in today's Scripture. He stated that if you say you love Him, then you'll do what He said.

Why? Because He forces you to? No. You obey Jesus because you love Him and you know He loves you. True love for God always results in our willingness to obey Him.

It doesn't mean you'll never sin, but it does mean you have a heart to obey God. This is God's plan for you. God desires that you fall so passionately in love with Him that you do whatever He asks.

What causes us not to obey God at times?

Ask God to build in your heart an attitude of love and trust.

DAY 3

John 14:16–18

The disciples were a little nervous about Jesus' announcement that He'd be leaving soon. In preparing His disciples for their ministry without Him, Jesus explained that the Father would send the Holy Spirit to live within them and that the Holy Spirit would always be with them to guide them. The word used for the Holy Spirit in verse 16 (Advocate) refers to someone who helps in times of trouble. In other words, the Holy Spirit will always be present to help you. Verse 17 called the Holy Spirit the "Spirit of truth." He'll always be there to guide you into truth. He's also the One who convicts you of sin, guides you in following God's direction for your life, and comforts you when you face difficult times. The Holy Spirit won't leave you—that's a promise!

What characteristic of the Holy Spirit best meets the greatest need in your life right now?

Thank God for sending His Holy Spirit to live inside you.

THE GIFT OF THE HOLY SPIRIT

DAY 4

John 14:25–26

These two verses mention two more aspects of the Holy Spirit, both of which are crucial for us as we continue our walk with Jesus. The Holy Spirit is with us and in us during the entire journey of our Christian lives. The Holy Spirit teaches us all the things we need to know to live the life God has created us to live. At different times He'll use the Bible, other believers, parents, ministers, teachers, our circumstances, and even our own thoughts to teach us.

Another role of the Holy Spirit is reminding us of what Jesus said. The Holy Spirit brings to our minds what we learn from the Bible and from spending time with Jesus. He also uses many different things in our lives to remind us of God's truths—and right when we need them. Having a daily walk with God allows you to hear Him better when He speaks to you through the Holy Spirit.

How often do you spend time in God's Word and in prayer? Time spent reading God's Word is vital because the Holy Spirit will bring the truths of God's Word back to your mind. Commit to reading God's Word and to praying daily.

DAY 5
John 14:27

Peace is another gift Jesus gives us through the Holy Spirit. In the midst of our problems or good times, the Holy Spirit brings peace to our lives if we continue to walk with Jesus. The word used here in the original language for peace means "inner rest and total well-being." So no matter what's happening around us, our trust in God can bring us inner rest because we know nothing can separate us from God. He's still in control, and God will never leave us. It's vital that we know this—or our problems could overwhelm us.

Are you going through a storm in your life right now?

Take your thoughts, fears, and worries to God. He already knows what your storms are. He's in control. Ask God to use whatever situations you go through—both good and bad—to honor His name and to strengthen your walk with Him.

WEEK 40
HE IS THE VINE

MEMORY VERSE:

"'I am the vine; you are the branches. If you remain in me and I in you, you will bear much fruit; apart from me you can do nothing.'" (John 15:5)

INTRODUCTION

God's Word contains His plan for living life the way it's designed to be lived. His Word is designed to bring about change in your life as you spend time reading it, studying it, and meditating on it. The Word forces you to choose between living life God's way or living life the way the world says it should be lived.

Godliness is basically devotion to God that results in a life that's pleasing to Him. That's a great definition, but what does devotion to God involve?

- *Realizing who our God really is. "Who among the gods is like you, O Lord? Who is like you—majestic in holiness, awesome in glory, working wonders?" (Exodus 15:11).*
- *Desiring and committing to know God. "My soul thirsts for God, for the living God. When can I go and meet with God?" (Psalm 42:2).*
- *Learning to love God. "Love the Lord your God with all your heart and with all your soul and with all your strength" (Deuteronomy 6:5).*

Some students assume being godly means being serious, wearing outdated clothes, having a holier-than-thou attitude, and following a long list of rules. That's not true. Godliness isn't based on a set of rules. It's based on a relationship. Godliness comes when we fall in love with Jesus. Then we learn about Him, see how He loves and accepts us, and realize that living for Him is what really matters.

This week we'll look at staying connected to Jesus. When that becomes a daily part of our lives, things begin to change.

DAY 1

John 15:1-4

If a branch is broken or cut off from the trunk of the tree, then it won't produce fruit; in fact, it will die. Jesus said believers are like that—if we don't stay connected to Him, then we'll die spiritually.

To stay connected to God—

- *Make spending time with God a priority in your life. Read His Word as part of your time with Him.*
- *Communicate with God throughout the day. You're always in His presence.*
- *Do what pleases God. Immediately obey what He shows you in His Word.*

Are you doing these things on a consistent basis?

Which of the above actions is most difficult for you?

What will you do to strengthen these three areas?

DAY 2

John 14:6; 15:5-8

Why would Jesus command us to abide in, live in, and stay connected to Him? Because Jesus is life. Without Him you'll never live the life you were created to live. Staying connected to Jesus will produce two powerful results in your life:

- *Powerful prayer. Your prayers will shift from asking for things for yourself to asking for things that will cause you to live for Christ. You'll ask God to use you to affect others for Him, to understand His Word, and to direct you. You'll really want to know, please, and honor God. God is then free to do great things with your life that bring Him honor.*
- *Fruit. Spiritual fruit isn't apples or oranges but godly characteristics—love, joy, peace, patience, kindness, goodness, faithfulness, gentleness, and self-control—and lives touched for God. You were made for this adventure. Why settle for less?*

Since you became connected with Jesus, what changes have you noticed in your life?

Pray that you'll stay connected to Jesus so you can live as God wants you to live.

DAY 3

John 15:9–11

What's the result of abiding in and staying connected to Jesus? One very important result is joy. Joy is a gladness of heart that comes from a deep confidence that God is in control of our lives. Jesus even told us that joy is made complete in us when we abide in Christ (v. 11).

Imagine complete joy. I believe that means that in every situation we keep experiencing God's joy—it remains throughout good or bad times.

Our joy is not only a great way to experience life for us, but it's also a way God works in the lives of the people around us. God uses our joy to attract others to Himself. People who don't know Christ just can't understand how we can be joyful even when we're hurting.

What's the difference between experiencing God's joy when we abide in Him and trying to be happy all the time?

How would the knowledge that God is in control of every area of your life help you have joy when things turn bad?

DAY 4

John 15:12-17

Jesus is clear that if we abide in Him, then there will be evidence of our relationship with Him. We've already looked at powerful prayer, fruit, and joy. A fourth evidence of our connection with Him is our love for others—especially other Christians.

Jesus showed us love by laying down His life for us. Although we may never be asked to lay down our lives for others, we'll be asked to give up our time, energy, and reputations. Remember, we're called to be servants just like Jesus (Mark 10:45).

Take another look at verses 16 and 17 of today's Scripture passage. God chose us to bear fruit. Take action today to do what you were chosen to do.

Is there an area of your life that needs to be pruned—an area that's preventing you from bearing fruit?

Spend time with God right now and talk to Him about this area.

DAY 5

John 15:18–25

Abiding in Christ has one difficult result: persecution. God's Word is very clear about this. If you choose to abide in Jesus, then you'll experience powerful prayer, you'll bear fruit, you'll have consistent joy, and you'll love others. But you'll also experience persecution from those who don't follow Jesus. So, don't be surprised when difficult times occur. Jesus told us to expect it, so it shouldn't surprise us. Remain connected to Him.

Write down the names of two people who hold you accountable in your walk with Jesus. Or ask God to bring to your mind two people (of the same sex as you) whom you'd like to hold you accountable.

Either thank them personally or ask them to help hold you accountable. Be willing to hold them accountable as well.

HIS BETRAYAL AND ARREST

MEMORY VERSE:

"So, if you think you are standing firm, be careful that you don't fall!"
(1 Corinthians 10:12)

INTRODUCTION

This week is exam time. Usually an exam is taken to test what you know—or don't know—about a subject. In this exam, we'll ask Jesus to examine our hearts to reveal anything we're allowing into our lives that could hurt our witness for Him.

God uses the Bible in our lives for a lot of reasons. Here are a few:

- *Lamp—it lights our way in a sin-darkened world (Psalm 119:105).*
- *Fire—it burns, consumes, and cannot be stopped (Jeremiah 20:9; Luke 24:32).*
- *Hammer—it can shatter hard hearts and break through closed minds (Jeremiah 23:29).*
- *Seed—it can take root in our lives and help us grow into a life that honors God (Matthew 13:18-23).*
- *Bread—it's necessary for spiritual life (John 6:51).*
- *Sword—it's our weapon in spiritual warfare (Hebrews 4:12; Ephesians 6:17).*
- *Milk—it contains simple truths that help young Christians grow (1 Peter 2:2-3).*
- *Mirror—it helps us see what we look like on the inside—our attitudes—and on the outside—our actions (James 1:23-25).*

This week ask God to use His Word to examine your heart.

1 Corinthians 10:12-13

God is waiting to do great things in your life if you'll surrender to Him. At the same time, there are forces that desire to make you ineffective for God. These forces have no authority over God. In fact, if you're a Christian, then these forces can influence you only if you choose to allow them to. God won't allow you to face anything that's too difficult for you.

The choice you make whether or not to obey God is the deciding factor. Paul challenged us to be careful not to fall. There is the possibility of falling if we don't choose the way God provides.

Begin this week by telling God you're giving Him the freedom to reveal anything in your life that would cause you to be ineffective for Him. Be ready to obey what He tells you to do.

DAY 2

Matthew 26:47-50

How many times have you thought, If I could just see Jesus face to face, then I'd never doubt Him and I'd always serve Him? Well, let's look at Judas.

Judas walked with Jesus for three years. He physically touched Jesus, talked to Him, and walked many miles with Him—and he still betrayed Jesus. Judas sat at Jesus' feet, heard Him teach, and prayed with Him. Judas ate meals with Jesus, laughed with Him, and cried with Him—and still sold Him out. Isn't that amazing?

Guess what? We're also capable of betraying Jesus by how we live. Standing firm for Jesus means realizing you will fall if you take your eyes off Him.

In what areas of your life do you feel the weakest?

What precautions will you take to avoid betraying Jesus in these areas?

If you've already fallen, then remember there is not one thing you've done that Jesus didn't already die for. So admit your failures to God (1 John 1:9). Then take precautions to be sure you don't slip into the same sins.

DAY 3

Matthew 26:51-54

The next precaution we must take in order to avoid sin is to realize who Jesus is. He doesn't need you to defend Him; He needs you to make obedience the first priority of your life. In verse 53 of today's passage, Jesus reminded Peter that He didn't need Peter to protect Him with his sword. All Jesus had to do was say the word, and twelve legions of angels would have come to His defense. (A Roman legion consisted of 6,000 soldiers, so Jesus was referring to an army of 72,000 angels!)

After all these weeks, do you realize whom you serve? He's the only and all-powerful God of the universe. He's able to step in and provide you with all the resources you need to stand firm—regardless of what happens in your life. But the choice to obey is up to you.

Write down a few of God's characteristics you've learned about thus far.

How will these characteristics provide you with all you need to stand firm?

Thank God for each of these characteristics as you talk to Him today.

DAY 4

Matthew 26:55-56

Despite knowing Jesus for three years—watching His awesome power in raising the dead, and hearing His words to Peter about twelve legions of angels waiting for His call—the disciples took off. When it got tough, verse 56 says "all the disciples deserted Him and fled."

Before, it appeared the disciples were strong. They really thought they were ready to stand with Jesus. They weren't. The power of Jesus was around them, but it wasn't in them.

Is it in you? Have you made the choice to follow Jesus? If not, then what's stopping you?

What will prevent you from betraying Jesus during times of temptation or difficulty? Jesus will remain faithful to you. Will you remain faithful to Him?

Tomorrow (like all days) will be a time of examination to see how strong you really are. Ask God to continue to reveal to you areas of weakness in your life and how to strengthen these weak areas.

DAY 5
Psalm 139:23–24

Begin this day by praying today's passage to God. Ask Him to examine your life and make the needed corrections.

Then pray over and answer the following:

- *How do I prioritize my time with God to make sure He's the main thing in my life?*
- *How will I expose myself to godly teaching and encouragement?*
- *How will I avoid getting caught up in things that don't matter?*
- *How will I let God use me to encourage other believers?*
- *How will I let God use me to reach the lost for Him?*
- *How can I learn to hate what God hates and love what God loves?*
- *How can I learn to deny myself, take up my cross, and follow Jesus?*
- *What am I allowing inside my mind, ears, and eyes that can hinder my walk with Jesus? And how will I prevent it from entering in the future?*

WEEK 42

THE CRIMINALS' QUESTIONS

MEMORY VERSE:

Greater love has no one than this: to lay down one's life for one's friends.
(John 15:13)

INTRODUCTION

Our God is an amazing God who's given us His words about life in the most amazing book of all time—the Bible. Along with wisdom on how to live life and how to come into a personal relationship with God through Jesus, it also contains these interesting but seldom-mentioned facts:

- *Forty-two thousand Ephramites died from a speech impediment (Judges 12:6).*
- *The shortest man in the Bible was Bildad the Shuhite—he was the height of a shoe (Job 2:11).*
- *Fools want to be beaten up (Proverb 18:6).*
- *Honesty is romantic (Proverb 24:26).*
- *Jesus drove a Honda Accord, but He didn't like talking about it (John 12:49).*
- *God created the world with His left hand. Jesus was sitting on His right hand (Ephesians 1:20).*

Okay, okay. I know that for some of these humorous "facts," you have to stretch the verse a little.

But one biblical fact that's certain is that Jesus willingly gave His life as a sacrifice. Sadly, many people either haven't heard the good news of the sacrifice of Jesus Christ or don't understand it. Our job and calling from God is to represent Jesus Christ to this generation.

This week our journey continues as we take a look at the sacrifice of Jesus.

DAY 1
John 15:13–14

What powerful verses! When God says He loves us, He backs it up with action. He showed us He loved us by dying for us.

Did you notice verse 14? Not everyone will experience the benefits of Jesus' sacrifice. Only those who obey His commands or act upon what He says will experience the forgiveness of sins. Guess what? You and I are called by God to tell the good news about Jesus' sacrifice to our generation.

Ask God to lay one person on your heart this week. Pray for an opportunity to talk to her about Jesus. Write her name in the Journal Space. Then act on the opportunity when it comes.

DAY 2

John 19:7

You've probably seen *The Passion of the Christ* or another movie about the crucifixion of Jesus. It's not a pretty sight. Jesus was whipped with braids of leather that had pieces of bone, metal, or glass fastened on the ends. These fragments would pierce the skin; and when the whip was pulled back, it would tear off pieces of flesh. The pain was more than one can imagine. Jesus was beaten, ridiculed, mocked, spat upon, and had a crown of long thorns mashed into His head. "Crucify Him!" was the cry of the crowd. Jesus' purpose was to die, and He did—in a way that was so painful that no person should have ever had to endure it.

But He did it—and He endured all of it for us.

Spend some time reflecting on the agony Jesus went through for you. Think about some of the sins you've purposely committed.

This pain—this passion of Jesus—is what He went through in order for you to experience God's forgiveness. Thank Him from the bottom of your heart.

DAY 3
John 19:8-16

What will you do with Jesus? What do your friends do when it comes to Jesus?

Pilate was faced with that decision. He knew Jesus claimed to be God, and he knew some people hated Jesus for making this statement (John 19:7). But Pilate was afraid of making a mistake. He was afraid of offending the Jewish leaders who wanted Jesus killed. He was afraid of killing an innocent man. He was afraid of the possibility that Jesus could be the Son of God. He was afraid of making the wrong decision as a leader of the people. Pilate washed his hands of the situation (both literally and figuratively) as a way of rationalizing what he allowed to happen to Jesus. As a result, Pilate became an accomplice in Jesus' death.

Just like Pilate, we have a choice to make. We know who Jesus is. We can choose to do nothing with that information, or we can take a stand and share this life-giving message with those around us.

Pray you'll have the courage not to wash your hands of Jesus this week but to share His love with others instead.

DAY 4

The crucifixion of Jesus always brings hurt to my heart. He paid for the forgiveness of my sins. Our salvation isn't free; it cost Jesus great suffering and pain. He became the bearer of the world's sin. Can you imagine the load of every sin ever committed being thrust upon the sinless person of Jesus Christ?

Read John 19:10. The horror of the crucifixion could have been avoided if Jesus had chosen that route. But He didn't. He willingly sacrificed Himself. What a great love our God has for us.

Have you shared with your friend (from Day 1 of this week) the great news of Jesus Christ?

DAY 5
John 19:38–42

Nicodemus responded to the death of Jesus by sacrificing his money, time, and reputation to honor Jesus. Since Nicodemus was a member of the Sanhedrin (the Jewish ruling council), it could have meant his expulsion, or possibly his death, if he were caught. Seventy-five pounds of myrrh and aloes was a huge and expensive amount that was usually reserved for royalty. Of course, Jesus was real royalty. Nicodemus responded with a total sacrifice.

How about you and me? What should be our response?

Will you accept this challenge to be committed to excellence, adventure, and daring as a disciple of Christ?

WEEK 43
HIS CRUCIFIXION

MEMORY VERSE:

"Yet to all who did receive him, to those who believed in his name, he gave the right to become children of God." (John 1:12)

INTRODUCTION

People respond to Jesus in different ways. I know a lady who encountered Jesus at a church service when she was a little girl. She's more than 70 years old now, and she still loves Him deeply. On the other hand, I once heard a man say, "The only thing that scares me more than thinking God doesn't exist is thinking He does." The man had completely turned his back on Jesus, pretending Jesus' life, death, and resurrection were some kind of fairy tale.

Jesus was mocked, abused, beaten, whipped, humiliated, and finally crucified for our sins in order that we might each have a personal relationship with God. You'd think people would respond with love and gratitude, but many don't. Even with the knowledge of what Jesus did for them, people still respond to Jesus in a variety of ways. Some accept Him; some reject Him with great indignity and abuse; others politely ignore Him.

Regardless of how people respond to Jesus, He still pursues them. He desires for them to come to Him and experience forgiveness, peace, and life—real life.

When we accept Jesus and begin to live for Him, we realize that life isn't what we thought it was. There's so much more to life that we have yet to experience. Jesus gives us a fulfilling and adventurous life here on earth—and an even greater life for all eternity with Him in heaven.

Let's take a look at Jesus, forgiveness, and life.

DAY 1
John 1:10-13

According to Romans 6:23, sin carries a payment: death. God dearly loves us, but our sin must be paid for. God's love led Him to take the form of a man—Jesus—live a sinless life, and make the payment for the sins of humanity. God's love and justice were satisfied in this way.

John 1:10-11 makes it clear: Many in the world will refuse this payment even though it's offered to them for free. How sad.

Verse 12 reassures us that anyone who chooses to receive Christ is given the right to be adopted into the family of God. Isn't that great news? And verse 13 reminds us that salvation isn't something one inherits, is born with, makes happen, or accomplishes. Only God gives salvation to those who ask to receive it.

Have you received Jesus into your life and asked Him to save you? If so, then write down the date, time, and place when this happened.

DAY 2

It's always interesting to watch how people respond to Jesus. When a person is near death, you'd think he would seek God and his forgiveness. Yet today's passage says one of the thieves who hung on the cross next to Jesus hurled insults at him. The thief's cry to Jesus to save him was actually his way of mocking Jesus. He was bitter about his own situation, and he acted on his bitterness by ridiculing Jesus.

Imagine this: The greatest act of love and sacrifice the world had ever seen was occurring right next to this thief. What was his response? Cruel words and insults. He was so close to Jesus on the cross; yet for all eternity he would be so far away.

How does your heart feel as you consider the thief's response as he watched the Son of God dying right next to him?

How do you feel knowing that many people around you may have this same attitude?

Tell God how you feel about Jesus' sacrifice of love on the cross for you.

DAY 3
Luke 23:40–42

One criminal hanging on a cross next to Jesus missed everything. Yet another, who had also lived a life of loss, gained everything at his final moment. How did this second thief respond? He admitted who he was—a person who deserved what he was getting, a person who had lived a life apart from God. He recognized who Jesus was and what He was able to do. But he didn't stop there. He also admitted he was helpless. He put his total faith in the only One who could save him. He repented of his sin by hoping in Jesus. At his last moment, he received eternal life.

How did Jesus respond to you when you cried out to Him for forgiveness and salvation?

How do you know?

Ask God to give you an opportunity to tell someone how Jesus Christ has changed your life.

DAY 4
Luke 23:43; 2 Peter 3:9

Jesus could have said to that second thief on the cross, "Sorry, but you waited too long. You've lived your entire life in sin, and now—at the very end—you come to me for forgiveness? Forget it!" But Jesus didn't respond that way.

Read 2 Peter 3:9 again. Jesus' love is so great that even at the last moment of the thief's life, Jesus still wanted him to respond to His invitation for eternal life. The thief was forgiven, and that very day he was with Jesus in paradise.

How deep and genuine is Jesus' love for you? How great is His desire to have a relationship with you? How consuming is His passion for you to experience forgiveness? So deep and consuming that He willingly gave His life for it. Anyone who calls to Jesus will be forgiven.

How should knowing the depth of God's love affect the way you live?

DAY 5
Luke 23:44-49

It was finished. Jesus' sacrifice for our sins was complete. Many who witnessed His crucifixion were never the same again. Some left quickly and seemed unchanged. Still others were drastically changed as they witnessed God's power in the days to come. The Scriptures you just read mention the responses of three people:

- *The centurion. After what he'd witnessed, he publicly admitted Jesus was surely "a righteous man" (or the Son of God, verse 47). The centurion was the officer in charge of the crucifixion, and he was changed forever.*
- *The crowd. All who had gathered to watch the crucifixion beat their chests and left. As the supernatural darkness fell, they realized they'd participated in a horrible crime against God.*
- *Those who knew Jesus. They stood off to the side and could only watch. (This is so much like us. We're often satisfied to remain on the sidelines and just observe.) Fortunately, this group was radically changed in the end.*

Which one of the three groups best describes you? Why?

Pray today you'll desire to be right with Jesus every step of the way.

HIS RESURRECTION

MEMORY VERSE:

"For what I received I passed on to you as of first importance: that Christ died for our sins according to the Scriptures, that he was buried, that he was raised on the third day according to the Scriptures." (1 Corinthians 15:3-4)

INTRODUCTION

How has your life changed since you gave it to Jesus? Many years ago I received an anonymous letter that showed the life change Jesus had brought about in a young high school student. The first paragraph was written nine months before she became a Christian, and the second paragraph was written a few months after she came to know Jesus.

> I sometimes wonder what it would be like to have people call my name and wave from across the cafeteria. I sit behind a cheerleader in my geometry class. One day I saw her with her mom at the mall. When I saw her, I forced a smile and said, "Hi." She said, "Hi," back, but in a real nonchalant way, then kept walking. "Who was that?" I heard her mom say. "I don't know," the cheerleader said. "Just somebody from class." People say God cares. I just wish He weren't the only one.

> In all the world there is nobody else like me. Since the beginning of time, there has never been another person like me. Nobody else has my smile. Nobody has my eyes, my nose, my hair, my hands, or my voice. I'm special. Nobody else anywhere has my taste for food or music or art. In all of time there's been no one who laughs like me or cries like me. I am special. I'm rare. And in all rarity, there is great value. I'm beginning to see that God created me for a very special purpose. Out of all the billions of applicants, only one is qualified for what God has for me to do. That one is me because I'm special!

Jesus brings about change in every life He enters.

DAY 1

1 Corinthians 15:1-8, 14

The resurrection of Jesus is the most important event in history. Verse 14 says if Jesus wasn't resurrected, then our faith would be useless. The entire Christian faith rests on the resurrection of Jesus. That's why the Scriptures tell us that more than 500 people saw Jesus after His resurrection. God left no doubt as to what happened.

It would have been so easy to crush Christianity before it even started. All one had to do was produce Jesus' dead body. No one could. If the disciples hid the body, then why were ten of them willing to die horrible deaths for preaching that Jesus had been resurrected? Why did no other historian at that time (secular or Jewish) dare to write that the resurrection was a hoax? Why did Christianity take off like a rocket and people flock to Jesus? Why did these scared disciples run away in fear during the crucifixion, yet become bold preachers after Jesus' resurrection? Because Jesus' resurrection actually happened.

What are some of your biggest questions about the resurrection?

Ask God to lead you to someone who loves Jesus and has knowledge of the Bible and the resurrection.

DAY 2

John 20:1-9

Isn't this an odd passage? After being with Jesus for three years, hearing Him talk about His coming resurrection, watching Him raise the dead to life, and witnessing the crucifixion—the disciples still had no clue.

They hid in fear until verse 19 (when Jesus appeared among them and showed them His pierced hands and side). Then they were excited because the evidence of Jesus' resurrection was there.

What evidence does your life show that Jesus rose from the dead, lives in you, and has forgiven and changed you?

Thank God today for the power of the resurrection in your life.

DAY 3
John 20:10-15

I love verse 10 in today's passage: The disciples went home. Have you ever thought the disciples ran from the empty tomb shouting with joy? That's not true. Peter and John went inside the tomb, saw no body, were confused, and went back to their homes. Amazing!

And where was faithful Mary Magdalene? Standing outside the tomb and crying because she thought someone had stolen Jesus. But when she looked back into the tomb, she saw two angels. Was she surprised, maybe even a little excited about seeing the angels? No, she simply told the angels that someone had stolen Jesus' body. She was still grieving. And her hurt was so great that even when she turned around and saw Jesus, she confused Him with the gardener. That's how life can be sometimes. Our hurt, our sin, and our difficulties cause us to lose sight of Jesus.

How could your hurt or difficulties cause you to lose sight of Jesus?

How does knowing that Jesus' power resides inside you make you feel?

DAY 4

One word and everything changed. Jesus just said her name: "Mary." He didn't make her feel guilty for not recognizing Him. He didn't criticize her for her lack of faith in Him. God Himself, in the form of Jesus, simply said her name, and her life changed forever. "Mary." She recognized His voice, turned to Him, and cried, "Rabboni!" (or "exalted teacher").

Through the resurrection Jesus teaches us how to live the life we're created to live. Through the adventure, danger, happiness, disappointments, and fulfillments in life, Jesus is speaking your name. He's calling you to follow Him—to allow Him to be the Teacher of your life.

Is there anything preventing Jesus from being the Teacher of your life?

DAY 5

John 20:17–20

What I love so much about Jesus is that wherever He goes, lives are changed. After Mary realized Jesus really had conquered death and was resurrected, her first reaction was to find the disciples and tell them the good news. When you grasp who Jesus really is—the awesome power He possesses and the forgiving love He dispenses—you just have to tell someone. The desire to share consumes you.

What is preventing you from walking with Jesus?

Spend some time with God right now and ask Him to show you anything that's keeping Him from being the Lord of your life. Yield that to Him.

HE RESTORED PETER

MEMORY VERSE:

"Humble yourselves before the Lord, and he will lift you up." (James 4:10)

INTRODUCTION

Before we begin this week's journey, let me ask you a few questions. Write yes or no beside each one.

Have you ever eaten sushi? _____
Have you ever ridden in a limousine? _____
Have you ever been bungee jumping? _____
Have you ever been white-water rafting? _____
Have you ever been scuba diving? _____
Have you ever been surfing? _____
Have you ever been snow skiing? _____
Have you ever been in a parade? _____
Have you ever walked into the wrong bathroom? _____
Have you ever thrown up on an amusement park ride? _____
Have you ever had your tonsils removed? _____
Have you ever worn braces? _____
Have you ever broken a bone? _____
Have you ever fainted? _____
Have you ever stayed up all night? _____
Have you ever had doubts about Christianity? _____

We could play "Have you ever?" all day long. But we're going to look at just one more "Have you ever?" question that everyone could answer "yes" to: Have you ever sinned?

This week our journey will take us to the deepest parts of our failures and back to the loving reach of Jesus.

DAY 1

James 4:7-10

These verses deal with pride. So many times we think, "I will never do that. I will never fall into that sin." In reality, there's nothing we wouldn't do if we were in the wrong situation, the wrong relationship, or if we let our guards down. Ephesians 6:10-18 reminds us that we're in a spiritual war. We have an enemy who hates God and hates us. God has given us a choice of whether or not to follow Him. What you do with that choice depends on what you allow into your mind and whom you allow into your heart.

God is telling you to humble yourself before Him—to realize you cannot make it without Him and to acknowledge Him as your strength. And never forget: He restores His relationship with you even after you've blown it.

What safeguards have you put into your life to help prevent things from entering your mind or your eyes that could hinder your relationship with God?

DAY 2

John 21:15–19

On the night before His death, Jesus predicted He'd be crucified and that all the disciples would forsake Him. But Peter arrogantly announced he'd never deny Jesus. Jesus replied that Peter would actually deny Jesus three times before the sun came up. And it happened just as Jesus said. Peter was devastated by his failure.

Shortly after Jesus' resurrection, He appeared to Peter and the other disciples. A beautiful act of restoration occurred as Jesus recommissioned Peter to God's service. Jesus asked Peter if he loved Him in both agape (commitment) and phileo (friendship). As Peter responded "yes," Jesus told Peter to feed (give spiritual nourishment to) and tend (love, be patient with, train) His sheep (other believers). Then Jesus said, "Follow me!"

After Peter failed Jesus at the most critical time in Jesus' life, Jesus didn't just forgive Peter; He restored him. He gave back to Peter his ministry of serving and strengthening other believers.

Do you feel as though you've let God down recently—as Peter did? How?

What are you waiting for? Come back to God right now and experience His love, forgiveness, and restoration.

DAY 3
John 21:20–22

We've already looked at today's passage earlier in our study, and it's worth studying again, because Peter was so much like us, wasn't he? Even after being restored, he still showed his selfish, impulsive side. He responded to Jesus by asking Him about the future of another disciple (John). It appears Peter wanted to be sure that John wouldn't get more than Peter would. Our old sinful nature is very difficult to shake. It probably will always be a battle—until we get to heaven.

How did Jesus respond? Did He scold Peter for his selfishness? No. Jesus said in verse 20, "If I want him to remain alive until I return, what is that to you? You must follow me." This is good advice for us also.

Ask God to help you focus on following Him, rather than on other believers' gifts or blessings.

DAY 4

1 John 1:7-22

Walking in the light will prevent us from sinning. We're always in God's presence, and all of God's power is in us as we walk in His ways. Obedience, trust, and time with God keep us aware of things that can enter our lives and trip us up.

We'll fail at times. And when we do, we need to confess our sins and return to God. He will restore our relationship with Him. It's not that our relationship with God is damaged (nothing can take that away), but unforgiven sin can affect our fellowship with Him.

When we make a mistake, Jesus still loves us and wants us to come back to Him—which is where we belong. As you pray, listen to God's Holy Spirit when He convicts you of sin so you can be made right with God again.

DAY 5

Genesis 3:1-10

In the first recorded game of hide-and-seek, Adam and Eve hid from God. They realized they'd sinned, and they hid. This was a pretty silly thing to do since God is omnipresent (everywhere) and omniscient (all-knowing).

When God found them, He jerked them out of their hiding place, yelled at them, and zapped them. Wrong! The first words out of God's mouth were, "Where are you?" Did God know where they were? Of course! But His desire was for Adam and Eve to come to Him and admit they'd sinned.

Isn't it amazing that God's first thoughts were of His relationship with Adam and Eve? As far as we know, they never did confess. Instead, they blamed each other, and then they blamed the serpent.

Where do you stand in your relationship with God right now?

Is there anything you need to do to improve it, based on what you just wrote?

Spend some time talking with God about it right now.

HIS CALL OF COMMISSION

MEMORY VERSE:

"Then Jesus came to them and said, 'All authority in heaven and on earth has been given to me. Therefore go and make disciples of all nations, baptizing them in the name of the Father and of the Son and of the Holy Spirit, and teaching them to obey everything I have commanded you. And surely I am with you always, to the very end of the age.'" (Matthew 28:18-20)

INTRODUCTION

What is the greatest gift God has given us in Jesus Christ? Life. John 1:4 says, "In him was life, and that life was the light of all mankind." It excites me to know God didn't give us religion, a set of rules to follow, or a philosophy about the world and life. He actually gave us life.

In fact, John 14:6 says Jesus is life. God gave us life. God gave us His words on how life is to be lived, and God sent Jesus to live it out for us.

Are you ready for life—real life? I'm talking about life that's so exciting, so fulfilling, and so full of joy and purpose that you just have to tell others about it. By watching you live this life, other people will experience a hunger for it in their lives. They'll begin to want what you have.

This life begins with a personal relationship with Jesus. It continues as you choose to live life as God planned it. But there are two things to consider here: First, it isn't easy; and second, only through the power of Jesus Christ living through you can you live life as God intends.

This week we'll allow Jesus to teach us how He's commissioned us to share His message of life with all people.

Acts 1:7-8

This week our journey will take us to the last words Jesus gave the disciples while He was on the earth. These words are also your mission. Jesus calls you to be a witness. A witness is someone who tells others what she has seen, heard, and experienced. You've witnessed good movies, songs, books, friends, activities, good teachers, bad teachers, great foods, bad foods, good times, and bad times. After you witness those things, you tell others about the experience.

Jesus is calling you to do the same—to tell others what you've experienced with Him.

How did you come to know Jesus?

How has Jesus changed your life?

DAY 2

Matthew 28:16

Now our journey gets exciting. Jesus was preparing to give His disciples the most important assignment anyone on the face of the earth had ever had. There were only eleven disciples (because Judas had committed suicide), and Jesus prepared them for their great commission by telling them to go to a certain mountain in Galilee. After all the disciples had seen Him, they didn't hesitate to obey.

Jesus desires that we learn to trust and obey Him as the beginning point of our great commission. He's asking us if we're willing to go where He tells us to go, do what He tells us to do, and speak to those He tells us to speak to. These are defining questions for us as we continue in our life journey with Jesus.

What's the biggest obstacle for you in being obedient to whatever Jesus tells you to do? Why?

Tell God what's on your heart today. Ask Him to help you do what He calls you to do. Tell Him you desire to yield all your rights to Him.

DAY 3

Matthew 28:17-18

Wasn't this an odd reaction from the disciples? In verse 17, all eleven disciples worshiped Jesus at the place where He'd told them to go. Yet even though they were actually with Jesus, some still doubted.

Imagine what would happen if the next time you and your youth group were worshiping, Jesus actually came down in the flesh and stood before you. Would you still have doubts? Some of Jesus' followers did. These guys weren't superstars. They were normal people like you and me.

So how did Jesus react to their doubts? Did He get upset with them? No. He told them all authority in heaven and earth was His. Since all authority and all power belong to Jesus, what are we scared of? We're free to do whatever He tells us. What are we waiting for?

How does knowing that Jesus has all authority affect the way you obey Him?

How does it affect other aspects of your life?

DAY 4

Matthew 28:19

So what is our commission from Jesus? We're commanded (not asked) and commissioned (assigned) to go to all peoples and all nations. To do what? To lead others to be followers of Jesus. Jesus has given us the greatest job in the world: Representing Jesus to the world and telling others what He can do in their lives.

Write the name of at least one person for whom you're praying to receive Christ.

Write some ways you can be involved in this person's life as a representative of Jesus.

Pray today that you'd be faithful to live for Jesus in that person's presence and share Jesus with him.

Wow! Our commission goes a little further than just telling others about Jesus, doesn't it? After our friends come to know Jesus, we're to be actively involved in helping them learn how to follow Him. We're to grow to the point where we can teach others how to walk with God on a daily basis.

God's plan is not that you simply sit in a Bible study or discipleship class and give all the right answers. He wants so much more for you. He wants you to live a life of excitement. He wants you to disciple others. He wants you to be actively involved in helping others grow in their relationships with Jesus. That's the way life gets even more exciting. Jesus says, "I will be with you wherever you go and in whatever you do—in both good and bad times." With a promise like that, what have we got to lose?

Pray first and then talk to your youth minister, Bible study teacher, pastor, or another mature Christian about preparing you to teach others how to grow in Christ. Ask them to help you fulfill the great commission that God has given us all.

Pray about this wonderful possibility.

HIS ASCENSION

MEMORY VERSE:

"'But you will receive power when the Holy Spirit comes on you; and you will be my witnesses in Jerusalem, and in all Judea and Samaria, and to the ends of the earth.'" (Acts 1:8)

INTRODUCTION

Being a part of fulfilling God's agenda in the world is pretty amazing. It's like being in God's movie. We get a small part in the movie of the history of Christianity in the world. Really! One day we'll watch the movie together, and we'll get excited when our part comes on the screen. Doesn't that sound great—our part?

God doesn't need us to fulfill His agenda (He can do it without us), but He chooses to invite us to play a part. What an honor! Your part is to yield your life to God—all the gifts, talents, and desires He's given you. In turn, God will use you to help others know and walk with Him. Then others will be able to live the exciting life God offers. It's not always easy, but it's always fulfilling.

Remember the research in Week 25's Introduction section? That 30-year study revealed how churchgoers were likely to outlive those who didn't go to church because they took better care of themselves. Of course, the research wasn't able to address the quality of a person's afterlife, but Jesus has already revealed that answer to us. While going to church won't change your eternal destiny, a relationship with Him certainly will. Plus, you and I have the honor of leading others to experience real life in Jesus.

Acts 1:1-3

Luke, the author of the book of Acts, was a physician. His analytical mind led him to be precise with the information he wrote. He wrote his two books to give the facts of Jesus' life and the early church. His purpose was that people would believe in Jesus and be encouraged to follow Him. These first few verses recap what has happened so far in the life of the early followers of Jesus.

Personally, I love verse 3. Luke mentions the "many convincing proofs" Jesus provided to help us know who He is so we will choose to believe in Him. These convincing proofs related to His resurrection. Our entire faith depends on the resurrection of Jesus, so He wanted to be sure that you and I know that the power that resurrected Jesus from the dead is the same power we have for telling others about Jesus.

What facts about Jesus are encouraging to you as you walk with Him each day?

DAY 2

Acts 1:4-5; 1 Corinthians 6:19; 2 Corinthians 1:21-22

God has a gift for you—it's Him. When you became a Christian, God put His Holy Spirit inside you. Your body became a temple of the Holy Spirit, so wherever you go, the Spirit goes with you. The Holy Spirit is not some scary, mysterious ghost. He is God. The Holy Spirit gives you the power to live the Christian life and understand how God's Word applies to you. He convicts you of sin and what will harm your spiritual walk. He comforts you and gives you compassion to share Jesus. What a great gift the Holy Spirit is!

Since you already have God living in you, what more do you need to walk with Jesus and share Him with others?

Thank God for the wonderful gift of the Holy Spirit in your life.

DAY 3

Acts 1:6–8

I firmly believe God is calling your generation to step out of your comfort zones and go where He leads beyond your school, home, city, and even state. God is calling people who have a desire for the nations to know Jesus. This could mean using your time and finances to go to a foreign country. He may call you to invest a week, a month, a summer, a few years, or your entire life in doing mission work. Are you willing to do so?

Your generation may be the one to bring the gospel to every people group in the world. What a privilege that would be! What is your part? Why don't you start by asking God about it?

Spend your time with God today asking for His will for you when it comes to missions. A part of His plan for you may involve the excitement of serving Him for a short term in another country. Then talk and pray about this with your youth minister or pastor.

DAY 4

After Jesus gave the disciples His final instructions and ascended to heaven, they were still staring intently at the sky. After what they'd just seen and heard, I think I would be, too. Then two angels appeared and basically said, "What are you looking at? He's coming back one day, so go do what He told you to do."

We can sit around all day waiting for Jesus and griping about how tough life is, or we can realize Jesus is coming back, and we have a job to do in the meantime. Guess what? We win in the end. Let's go out and tell as many as we can about Him!

What are some ways you could be a witness for Christ in your home, at your school, where you work, or in other places that are a part of your routine?

Pray for God to give you opportunities to share Jesus.

DAY 5
Acts 1:12-15

After all the disciples had seen and heard, what did they do next? They joined with others and began to pray. Prayer was vital for them, and it's vital for us. Verse 15 states there were only about 120 believers at that time. Yet God used that small number to bring the message of Jesus around the world. Imagine what He'll do through your group of Christian friends if you're willing to let God use you. Are you willing? What are you committed to doing on a daily basis in order to achieve this purpose of taking the gospel to your school and your community—and to the entire world?

Talk with a few of your Christian friends about getting together before school on a consistent basis to pray for your school.

Talk to a few of your Christian friends about getting together for 30 minutes on Sunday mornings to ask God to move in your church. Write down the names of the friends you'll discuss this with. Pray for them as well.

HIS PROMISED RETURN

MEMORY VERSE:

"He who testifies to these things says, 'Yes, I am coming soon.' Amen. Come, Lord Jesus." (Revelation 22:20)

INTRODUCTION

What would you say if you knew you had only a few more minutes to live? What would you say if you were lying on your deathbed with friends and family gathered around you, and you knew that whatever you said next would be your final words on this planet?

Many times I've sat with people in their last days. When they look at me and say, "I want to tell you something," they have my complete attention. It's so interesting to hear what they have to say and why. You'd think a person's final words would be of extreme importance and show what they really value.

Let's take a quick look at the last words of a few famous people:

"See in what peace a Christian can die."
—Joseph Addison, writer (d. 1719)

"Am I dying or is this my birthday?" —Lady Nancy Astor (d. 1964)

"How were the receipts today at Madison Square Garden?"
—P.T. Barnum, entrepreneur (d. 1891)

"I have tried so hard to do the right."
—Grover Cleveland, U.S. President (d. 1908)

"Don't you dare ask God to help me."
—Joan Crawford, actress (d. 1977)

"All my possessions for a moment of time."
—*Elizabeth I, Queen of England (d. 1603)*

"It is very beautiful over there."
—*Thomas Edison, inventor (d. 1931)*

"Nothing matters. Nothing matters."
—*Louis B. Mayer, film producer (d. 1957)*

"Lord help my poor soul." —*Edgar Allan Poe, writer (d. 1849)*

"I die hard but am not afraid to go."
—*George Washington, U.S. President (d. 1799)*

"I have offended God and mankind because my work did not reach the quality it should have." —*Leonardo da Vinci, painter-sculptor-inventor-scientist-engineer (your basic off-the-charts genius) (d. 1519)*[1]

What do you think Jesus' final words would be?

This week we'll spend a little time looking at the last recorded words of Jesus. What a way to finish out the year! Are you ready?

---

1 "Dying Words: The last words spoken by famous people at death, or shortly before," in Brain Candy Celebrity Quotes, www.corsinet.com/braincandy/dying. html (accessed October 16, 2007).

DAY 1

Revelation 22:12-13

Jesus' final words to us began with the word behold. It's a powerful word that's a formal or fancy way of saying "LISTEN!" In other words, what's coming next is extremely important, so listen closely.

After grabbing our attention, Jesus said He's coming soon. This is the second time in Revelation chapter 22 that He warns us of His second coming (the first time is in verse 7). So it's obvious He wants us to realize this fact—He is coming.

Write down your first thoughts about how you feel knowing that Jesus is coming back.

Why do you feel this way about His coming?

What did Jesus say He'll do when He comes? He'll hold us accountable for what we've done with our lives. Your salvation is based on your response to Jesus, but He'll judge Christians based upon our works for Him. Verse 13 reminds us of who He is and the reason He has the right to serve as Judge.

Do you really know Jesus? If not, then ask Him to come into your life right now and forgive your sins.

If you do know Jesus, then spend some time in prayer yielding all to God and asking Him to give you opportunities to tell someone about Jesus this week.

DAY 2

Revelation 22:14-15

Congratulations! You've just read the very last beatitude (blessing) in the Bible! Jesus gave it to us because He is coming soon. The phrase "those who wash their robes" refers to people who've asked Jesus to be their Savior. They've washed their robes in Jesus' blood, which means they've accepted Jesus' payment for their sins. Now Jesus gives them eternal life (tree of life) and the right to enter heaven (the city of God).

Take a minute to pray. Thank Jesus for His sacrifice and His forgiveness.

The next verse is a reality check. Some people won't go to heaven. The word dogs is a Greek word, *kuon*,[1] and it's generally used to represent those who have impure minds. In other words, these people didn't follow the proper rules for cleansing as required by Jewish law. They weren't allowed to worship in the temple. These people refuse to accept God's forgiveness and salvation through Jesus (John 14:6; Acts 4:12). What these people practice (do continually) will be revealed.

Yes, there really is a hell. There is a consequence for not trusting Jesus as your Lord and Savior. As we head toward the end of our year spent together in God's Word, ask God, again, to put on your heart the names of five people who don't know Jesus. Write them down and commit to pray for them on a daily basis.

---

1 Thayer and Smith, "Greek Lexicon entry for Kuon" in *The KJV New Testament Greek Lexicon* (Crosswalk.com) http://www.biblestudytools.net/Lexicons/Greek/grk.cgi?number=2965&version=kjv (accessed October 16, 2007).

DAY 3

Revelation 22:16

Oxymorons (two words that contradict or don't fit together) are fun to discover. Here are some of my favorites:

- *Act naturally*
- *Found missing*
- *Good grief*
- *Terribly pleased*
- *Pretty ugly*
- *Tight slacks*
- *Clearly misunderstood*
- *Alone together*
- *Same difference*
- *Now then…*

In today's verse Jesus used an oxymoron to show you who He really is. "The root [beginning or foundation] and the offspring of [follows after or birthed through] David" is a reminder that Jesus is the Messiah, the Chosen One, our Savior, and God with us. "The bright Morning Star" was a clear statement to the Jewish people that Jesus is the Messiah who will deliver and direct His people like a star. Jesus clearly said He is God, our salvation, all-powerful.

Jesus asked His disciples, "Who do you say I am?" (See Matthew 16:13-16.) Peter responded, "You are the Messiah, the Son of the living God" (v. 16). "Christ" is not Jesus' last name. It's His title. He is Jesus the Christ, Jesus the Messiah, Jesus the Chosen One.

Write as many different names or descriptions of Jesus as you can remember.

Go over the list of names you've written for Jesus. Praise Jesus for who He is. Guess what? One day you and I will be praising Him face to face.

DAY 4

Revelation 22:17

This verse is John's response to Jesus' statement that He's coming soon.

I love weddings, especially when the back doors of the church open and the bride comes down the aisle. This is usually the groom's first look at his bride in her wedding dress. Next time you're at a wedding, keep your eyes on the groom as the doors open. His expression will be classic.

That's not how a Jewish wedding began. Jewish custom required the groom to choose his most loyal friend (best man), and the two of them would go to the bride's home. She'd be dressed and ready, and then the groom and best man would escort her to the temple for the wedding ceremony.

Did you catch that? Bride, be ready because the Groom is coming for you! Jesus calls believers (the church) the "bride of Christ." That means He's coming for us! So we need to be ready.

Turn back to verse 12 and read it again. Jesus is coming! What is our response? "Come on, Jesus! We're ready!"

What's the most difficult part about knowing that Jesus is coming soon, yet still having to wait for Him?

DAY 5

Revelation 22:18–20

Our final look into God's Word contains a warning and a strong reminder. We're warned not to add or take away from what's written in the Bible. This verse is not just for the book of Revelation (read Deuteronomy 12:32) but for the entire Bible. Watch out for people who claim to have a new word from Christ. John warned us of the terrifying results.

Ask God to give you wisdom so you won't be fooled by those who attempt to lead you away from the truth of God's Word. God is not bound by time as you and I are; His Word is as relevant for living life today as it was 2,000 years ago.

Jesus spoke for the last time in the New Testament—"Yes, I am coming soon!" Jesus could come back at any moment. But even if He delays, you could still die at any moment and meet Jesus face to face. Are you ready?

Spend some time in prayer. Ask God to show you areas of your life where you aren't ready and what action you need to take. Write these down as God brings them to your mind. Then obey Him and make the necessary changes.

Even so, come Lord Jesus!

A FINAL WORD

Real life begins with Jesus. Until a person finds Jesus, she isn't really living. Jesus is the Focus of all history, but He's also the Author of all life. Romans 10:9 says, "If you declare with your mouth, 'Jesus is Lord,' and believe in your heart that God raised him from the dead, you will be saved." Jesus bought us by His death on the cross. And salvation is as simple as believing—placing our confidence and trust—in Jesus Christ.

Forty-eight weeks ago, I asked: "Do you know Jesus?" By now I hope you know more about Jesus than when we began our journey together. But the purpose of working through this journal has not been to learn more about Jesus. The purpose has been for you to know Jesus better.

There's a world of difference between knowing about Jesus (by studying His Word and reading the inspiring stories told by His followers) and really knowing Him (by actually spending time with Him). Knowing Jesus Christ means allowing Him to open your heart to His Holy Spirit and being obedient to what He tells you to do. Knowing Jesus means developing a love relationship with Him that will last for eternity.

Jesus has equipped you for real life. God's power is available to you as a believer through the Holy Spirit. Jesus purchased your freedom from the death penalty for your sins through His own excruciating death on the cross. And you have eternal life through Jesus' resurrection.

God has called you to be different: You're to live a life of love and worship toward God that overflows from a heart of gratitude. You're to love your brothers and sisters in Christ as a demonstration of your love for God. And you're to share the love of God with those who don't know Him.

Allow God to take control of your life...and hold on for the ride!

Johnny Derouen

22157220R00163

Made in the USA
Columbia, SC
27 July 2018